The Role of Business in the Modern World

D0964061

The Role of Business in the Modern World

Progress, Pressures and Prospects for the Market Economy

DAVID HENDERSON

FOREWORD BY GEORGE KAILIS

The Institute of Economic Affairs

First published in Great Britain in 2004 by
The Institute of Economic Affairs
2 Lord North Street
Westminster
London sw1p 3lb
in association with Profile Books Ltd

The mission of the Institute of Economic Affairs is to improve public understanding of the fundamental institutions of a free society, with particular reference to the role of markets in solving economic and social problems.

A CIP catalogue record for this book is available from the British Library.

isbn 0 255 36548 9

Many IEA publications are translated into languages other than English or are reprinted. Permission to translate or to reprint should be sought from the Director General at the address above.

Typeset in Stone by MacGuru Ltd
info@macguru.org.uk

Printed and bound in Great Britain by Hobbs the Printers

CONTENTS

THE AUTHOR

David Henderson was formerly (1984–92) head of the Economics and Statistics Department of the Organisation for Economic Cooperation and Development (the OECD) in Paris. Before that he worked as an academic economist in Britain, first in Oxford (Fellow of Lincoln College) and later in University College London (Professor of Economics); as a British civil servant (first as an Economic Adviser in HM Treasury, and later as Chief Economist in the UK Ministry of Aviation); and as a staff member of the World Bank. In 1985 he gave the BBC Reith Lectures, which were published in book form under the title of *Innocence and Design: The Influence of Economic Ideas on Policy* (Blackwell, 1986).

Since leaving the OECD he has been an independent author and consultant, and has acted as Visiting Fellow or Professor at the OECD Development Centre (Paris), the Centre for European Policy Studies (Brussels), Monash University (Melbourne), the Fondation Nationale des Sciences Politiques (Paris), the University of Melbourne, the Royal Institute of International Affairs (London), the New Zealand Business Roundtable, and the Melbourne Business School. Among his recent publications is *Anti-Liberalism 2000* (IEA, London, 2001). He is an Honorary Fellow of Lincoln College, Oxford, and in 1992 he was made Commander of the Order of St Michael and St George.

FOREWORD

Corporate Social Responsibility is a booming area. In April 2004 a Web search for the term Corporate Social Responsibility (CSR) returned over two million hits. Simplistic notions of CSR can be seen as the salvation for all problems facing business and society. But what kind of a solution is this? The American journalist and critic H. L. Mencken once stated that 'for every complex problem, there is a solution that is simple, neat, and wrong'. CSR gives the appearance of a comprehensive solution but, as Professor David Henderson outlines, it fails to deliver.

In inviting Professor Henderson to Australia to give the Lang Hancock Public Lecture I challenged him to go beyond criticism of CSR. My institution, the University of Notre Dame Australia, is a young private university founded to advance learning and the professions within a context of Catholic faith and values. Many of our supporters are business and professional people of good conscience with a strong interest in social issues. A critique of CSR that failed to clarify a positive role for business would leave these community leaders uncertain and dissatisfied. In addition, only a positive role, clearly defined, represents an adequate answer to those who would use CSR to question the legitimacy of business enterprises as contributors to society.

In responding to the challenge, Professor Henderson sets current issues in a broad historical perspective. He argues that the primary role of business enterprises, which has not changed, is to act as vehicles of innovation and economic progress, and that the effective performance of that role has never depended, and does not now depend, on a commitment by businesses to further the public interest or to pursue 'sustainable development'. The business contribution results from the combination of opportunities and pressures that only freely functioning markets can provide. Public action to extend the scope and improve the functioning of markets is still the principal way to ensure that businesses contribute to the general welfare.

One of the highlights of this book is that Professor Henderson directly addresses fashionable criticisms of business in relation to globalisation and economic liberalisation. Myths abound on these issues that are not supported by either cogent economic reasoning or sound statistical evidence. His work navigates the dangers of oversimplification on the one hand, without resorting to an arid style that speaks only to the economic specialist on the other.

Business is a creative endeavour contributing to the development of society; it is tempered by competition and bound within the rule of law. CSR risks becoming yet another fashionable notion that fails to deliver long-term benefits but distracts businesses from pursuing their proper and vital economic role. Professor Henderson has issued a clear challenge to proponents of CSR to go beyond platitudes and put up stronger and more cogent arguments for public debate.

GEORGE KAILIS

Professor of Management
Dean, College of Business
The University of Notre Dame, Australia

As in all IEA publications, the views expressed in Hobart Paper 150 are those of the author and not those of the Institute (which has no corporate view), its managing trustees, Academic Advisory Council members or senior staff.

EDITORIAL NOTE

The Role of Business in the Modern World is the 150th Hobart Paper to be published by the Institute of Economic Affairs. The Hobart Papers are the longest-established of four main series of papers currently published by the IEA.

The purpose of the Hobart Papers is to contribute a stream of authoritative, independent and readable commentary to the discussion of economic opinion and policy. The first of this series was *Resale Price Maintenance and Shoppers' Choice* by B. S. Yamey, which opened the way to the revolution in retailing that has transformed the lives of every one of us. Others have illuminated such issues as rent control, labour market restrictions, the increasing regulation of corporate governance, state control of health and education, taxation, and the land use planning system. Indeed, there is hardly an aspect of public policy that has been safe from exposure to rigorous scrutiny by IEA authors. Many have proposed policies that seemed beyond the bounds of the politically possible at the time they were written but have become part of mainstream economic thinking and political reform.

The 150th Hobart Paper, by David Henderson, follows in this tradition. Capitalism is under attack from those who would like to redefine the role of business in such a way that it would be, once again, subject to control by political rather than economic forces. Opinion formers and policy-makers in past decades took note of the message of earlier Hobart Papers in order to develop policies that promoted a free and prosperous economy after the post-war experiment with central planning. Their modern contemporaries urgently need to ponder Professor Henderson's message if they are to protect the free society from its modern enemies.

ACKNOWLEDGEMENTS

My thanks are due to Notre Dame University, and in particular to Professor George Kailis, Professor of Management there, for the invitation to give the Lang Hancock Lecture and for their kind hospitality in Fremantle. For their helpful comments on various drafts, I would like to thank Jonathan Brooks, Ian Castles, Greg Dwyer, Paul Hare, George Jones, George Kailis, Alfred Kenyon, Roger Kerr, Sir Geoffrey Owen, Colin Robinson, David Sawers, Maurice Scott and Simon Scott. Most of the work of preparing and revising the text was carried out at the Westminster Business School where I hold a Visiting Professorship. Once again, my thanks and acknowledgements are due to the School and to its Head, Professor J. R. Shackleton.

SUMMARY

- It is now widely held that a new era has just dawned, in which businesses need to adopt a new conception of their mission, purposes and conduct, by endorsing and putting into effect the doctrine of 'Corporate Social Responsibility' (CSR). They are urged to embrace 'corporate citizenship', and to conduct themselves, in conjunction with an array of 'stakeholders', so as to further the cause of 'sustainable development' by pursuing a range of social and environmental goals.

- Over the past half-century or more, economic progress across the world as a whole has been strikingly rapid by all previous standards. Recent experience has confirmed that the material progress of people everywhere, rich and poor alike, depends above all on the dynamism of the economies in which they live and work, and that rapid progress is now to be expected wherever the political and economic conditions exist for a market economy to operate effectively.

- As in the past, the principal *direct* impulse to economic progress in recent decades has come from profit-related activities and initiatives on the part of business enterprises working within the framework of a competitive market economy. This business contribution results from the twin stimuli that a market economy provides: wide-ranging *entrepreneurial opportunities* and pervasive *competitive pressures*. The two aspects are inseparable, since the competitive pressures arise from market opportunities that are themselves opened up by economic freedom.

- From an economy-wide perspective, now as in the past, the primary *role of business is to act as a vehicle for economic progress*. This role is not, and cannot be, 'internalised' by enterprises themselves. Economic progress does not depend on a commitment by businesses to bring it about.

- Globalisation has not transformed the primary role of business, as the advocates of CSR maintain. On the contrary, it has confirmed and reinforced it.

- Despite the clear record of economic progress, alarmist beliefs about the situation and prospects of the world are widely held, today as in the past: they make up a *global salvationist* consensus. This consensus has gained ground in recent years as a result of the spread of mistaken ideas about the nature and effects of globalisation, the rise of radical egalitarianism, and concerns about the possibility and the associated risks of global warming. The main single factor, however, has been the endorsement, by governments as well as elements of public opinion, of sustainable development as a goal.

- In a well-functioning market economy, enterprise profits are performance-related: they are earned by providing consumers with products and services that they wish to buy, and doing so in a resourceful and innovative way. Profits can thus serve as an indicator of each enterprise's contribution to the welfare of people in general. As such, they provide an indispensable economic signalling function. How well they serve this purpose depends on how far they are in fact performance-related. This in turn depends largely on the extent of competition and economic freedom.

- To emphasise the primary role of business, and with it the signalling function of performance-related profits, is not to imply that ethical considerations have no place in the business world. Today, as always, profit-oriented businesses have moral as well as legal obligations. In relation to the complex issues of enterprise and individual conduct that arise in business, as also those of corporate governance, the doctrine of CSR has little or nothing to contribute. Much of the thinking that underlies it betrays the age-old obsession with the purity of motives, together with a failure to understand the role of performance-related profits. Profits are viewed as a means to higher ends, through providing room for virtuous conduct, rather than as a possible indicator of an enterprise's contribution to the general welfare.
- It may be true, or become true, that businesses will increasingly have little choice but to take the path of CSR, in the interests of profitability or even survival. But its general adoption, whether from social pressures or legal requirements, would do more harm than good. The case against CSR is not that it would necessarily be bad for profits, but that, whatever its effects on enterprise profitability in particular cases, it would make people in general worse off.
- It is not through transforming enterprise goals and conduct, in the ways suggested by CSR adherents, that the business contribution to the general welfare can be improved, but through actions by governments that would serve to reinforce the primary role of business. Such actions have to be directed

to widening market opportunities and increasing competitive pressures. Their aim and effect is to increase economic freedom. The key element is *liberalisation*.

- In today's world, there is everywhere ample scope for further liberalisation. From the end of the 1970s, though with exceptions and many local variations, economic policies across the world became on balance more market-oriented. But collectivist ideas and anti-market pressures remain influential everywhere: there was and is no 'neo-liberal hegemony'. On the contrary, the future scope and status of the market economy are put in question by today's *new millennium collectivism*.

- The main headings for liberalisation now include: greater freedom of international trade and investment flows; further privatisation, through arrangements that will promote free entry and competition; opening up to competition the provision of goods and services that are made available largely or entirely at public expense; 'marketisation', i.e. charging people, whether as individuals or as voters, for what are now free or heavily subsidised goods and services; and deregulation under many headings, including reversal of the general trend towards eroding freedom of contract.

- Two rival diagnoses of the status of capitalism and the market economy are on offer. On the one hand, it is argued that socialism is now finally discredited, and that the choice between more or less market-directed forms of capitalism in democratic societies is not a fundamental one. A contrary view is that collectivist influences within these societies could well pose a threat to prosperity and economic freedom. There are good arguments on both sides. Even on the first hypothesis, however, the case for further liberalisation remains valid.

- Measures and policies that narrow the scope of markets and reduce economic freedom can do extensive harm. Not only do they act as a brake on economic progress, but they are liable to impair the quality of individual and social life. A well-functioning market economy gives people the freedom to act in ways that will make their lives more complete, as well as materially richer.

PREFACE

This essay is a revised and greatly expanded version of the text that I used as a basis for delivering the Lang Hancock Lecture at the University of Notre Dame in Fremantle, Western Australia, in December 2002. In adapting and building on the original text, I have retained in places the relatively informal and personal style of a lecture. This is partly in the interests of readability, but also because I am conscious of having dealt with a complex set of issues in a summary way.

The Notre Dame University lecture series commemorates a notable Australian businessman. Lang Hancock (1909–92) played a leading role, right from the start, in the discovery, exploration and development of what became revealed as the immense iron ore deposits of the Pilbara region of Western Australia. In what had been a remote, desolate and virtually uninhabited area, an industry has grown up which in 2002 shipped out 175 million tonnes of ore. In revising my lecture text I took out most of the specifically Western Australian allusions; but I have kept in the main references to Hancock, since he can be seen as a local instance of a worldwide phenomenon. His career exemplifies the entrepreneurial role in promoting innovation and economic progress within a market-led economy.

The Role of Business in the
Modern World

Business is not to be thought of as lying at a lower level of human concerns than the writing of fiction or the seeking of power through political pretensions. Business is creative, and its study is as worthy of human effort as that of history, law, medicine, social organization and art.

G. L. S. SHACKLE, *EPISTEMICS AND ECONOMICS: A CRITIQUE OF ECONOMIC DOCTRINES*, IN THE INTRODUCTION TO THE 1992 EDITION PUBLISHED BY TRANSACTION BOOKS, P. XII

... since 1978, Chinese performance has been transformed by liberalisation of the economy.

ANGUS MADDISON, *THE WORLD ECONOMY: A MILLENNIAL PERSPECTIVE*, OECD DEVELOPMENT CENTRE, 2002, P. 146

1 SETTING THE SCENE

Background

This book's main theme is the role of business in the modern world. I consider both the contribution of business enterprises to the general welfare and their social responsibilities. Under the latter heading, I offer both a critique of some widely held current views on the subject and an alternative approach. I argue that the primary role of business enterprises has not changed: now as in the past, its performance depends, not on the resolve of their directors and managers to contribute to the public welfare, but on their being part of a competitive market economy. I outline ways in which this primary role could now be further strengthened, through economic policies which extend the scope and improve the functioning of markets. Finally, I review the situation and prospects of capitalism and the market economy today.

As noted in the Preface, the essay has its origins in the Lang Hancock Lecture which I gave at the University of Notre Dame in Fremantle, Western Australia, in December 2002. The invitation to deliver the lecture came from George Kailis, Professor of Management at Notre Dame, and in the letter of invitation he made a challenging proposal as to its subject matter. The story is as follows.

A few years ago, to my surprise, I became interested in, and concerned about, some influential current trends of thinking about the role and responsibilities of businesses in the modern world. It is now held by many, both in the business milieu and more generally, that companies everywhere, whatever the nature of their business, should redefine their role and objectives, their corporate mission. They should endorse the notion of 'Corporate Social Responsibility' (CSR for short), and run their affairs accordingly. The more I learned about this newly arisen way of thinking, the more worrying I found it; and eventually I wrote a short book on the subject, entitled *Misguided Virtue: False Notions of Corporate Social Responsibility*. The book was first published in mid-2001 by the New Zealand Business Roundtable, and later in that year issued in London by the Institute of Economic Affairs. The London version contains an additional chapter in which, among other things, I comment on the way in which the notion of CSR has been formally endorsed by the European Commission.

Misguided Virtue is a frontal attack on CSR which has brought me notoriety in some business circles. In a recently published book of close to 300 pages, written by the chief executive officers (CEOs) of three leading companies and issued under the auspices of the World Business Council for Sustainable Development (WBCSD), one and a half pages are specifically devoted to refuting what I am alleged, misleadingly, to have said.[1] When the book appeared, I made a public offer to the authors to prepare for them, for an agreed fee, also in one and a half pages, a critique of my argument that would be both more accurate and more powerful than theirs;

---

1   Charles O. Holliday, Stephan Schmidheiny and Philip Watts, *Walking the Talk: The Business Case for Sustainable Development*, Greenleaf, Sheffield, 2002. The supposed refutation is on pp. 105–7.

but the offer has not been taken up.[2] In view of the claims made for this publication – it is described on the dust jacket as 'the most important book on corporate social responsibility yet published' – and because the WBCSD which sponsored it now has a membership of over 170 large international companies across the world, I refer to it at a number of points below. It presents a view of the world, and of the changing role of companies within it, that is widely held in business circles today.

In his letter, George Kailis wrote: 'I share many of the criticisms expressed in your work about "Corporate Social Responsibility"'; he went on to say, however: 'The topic I would be interested in you speaking on is going further and outlining the "proper role for business"'. This suggestion was so manifestly reasonable as to be impossible to resist; and together we agreed accordingly on what form the lecture should take. But in taking this proposed course, I was – and remain – conscious of having accepted a formidable challenge. I do not pretend to offer now a full and rounded treatment of the subject. Here as in the original lecture, what I have to say is personal and exploratory.

Introducing CSR

By way of preliminary, let me give a brief sketch of what is meant by CSR and what is implied by a commitment to it, drawing on some of its standard terms and phrases.

---

2 The offer was (and remains) subject to two conditions: (1) that in any public use of or reference to my text, the authorship should always be attributed, and (2) that such use should be accompanied by a statement that, despite having volunteered this critique of *Misguided Virtue*, I stand by everything that I said in the book.

The doctrine of CSR is seen by its many adherents as a creative response by business enterprises to problems and challenges that have been thrown up by recent changes on the world scene. According to the doctrine, businesses should now consciously endorse the notion of 'corporate citizenship'. In giving effect to it, they should run their affairs in close conjunction with an array of interested 'stakeholders': they should practise 'multiple stakeholder engagement'. Corporate citizenship chiefly involves pursuing the goal of 'sustainable development'. This goal is taken to have three dimensions – economic, environmental and social. Hence companies are enjoined to set objectives, measure their performance, and have that performance independently audited and reported on, in relation to all three: they should aim to meet the so-called 'triple bottom line'.[3] By following this course, they will both promote the general welfare and be seen to do so. Only through such actions (it is said) can businesses respond to what are now 'society's expectations', and thus earn and keep their informal 'licence to operate'. In so responding lies the key to long-run commercial success, since profits depend to a large extent on reputation, which itself now depends on being seen to have done the right thing by promoting sustainable development in all its aspects. In today's world, therefore, virtuous corporate conduct will bring its own reward: in taking the path of CSR, businesses will improve their long-run profitability. They will likewise improve the working of the market economy, which left to itself,

---

3   There is an ambiguity here relating to the word 'social', which is commonly used in both a wider and a narrower sense. In the term 'corporate social responsibility' it refers to all three supposed dimensions of sustainable development. But it is also applied more narrowly to one of these dimensions only – i.e. the 'social', as opposed to the 'economic' and the 'environmental'.

with companies typically concerned only with short-term financial gains, would give too little weight to the environmental and social considerations which now enter into 'society's expectations'. The general adoption of CSR, by businesses around the world, will 'give capitalism a human face'.[4]

CSR is a radical doctrine. It points to far-reaching changes in business thinking and practice. How far the many firms that have formally signed up to it have turned a genuinely new leaf is not clear, and no doubt there are those among them for whom its adoption is no more than a prudent concession to outside opinion, not to be taken too seriously. But for the many true supporters of CSR, within the business world and elsewhere, it offers a new blueprint for business aims and conduct. They believe that what is involved is nothing less than 'corporate transformation' (*Walking the Talk*, p. 126). In the words of one of the companies that has endorsed the doctrine wholeheartedly, the Royal Dutch/Shell Group, the commitment to CSR 'demands a deep shift in corporate culture, values, decision-making processes and behaviour'.[5]

In this book I present a critique of CSR, and the ways of thinking that go with it, which draws on the argument of *Misguided Virtue* but also extends it. In returning to the subject, I have brought in four further elements in particular. First, the critique is now set in a broad historical context, covering the evolution

4 Guidance on what CSR means and involves is given in three publications of the WBCSD. First is a draft report, entitled *Corporate Social Responsibility*, issued in 1999. Second is the final version of this draft, published in 2000 under the title *Corporate Social Responsibility: Making good business sense*. Both these reports were published in Geneva by the WBCSD itself, and I comment on both in *Misguided Virtue*. The third and most recent source is *Walking the Talk*, which I comment on at various points below.

5 The quotation is from a 1998 Shell report entitled *Profits and Principles – does there have to be a choice?*

both of the world economy and of ideas and opinions relating to the course of economic change. Second, I have commented more explicitly on issues of business conduct and motivation. Third, the critique goes together with a positive message: I suggest how 'the proper role for business' can best be viewed and defined, and I outline ways in which governments today can help to ensure that the role is more effectively performed. Last, I review the changing fortunes of capitalism and the market economy over the period since the end of World War II, and consider the widely held view that capitalism has now finally triumphed over its enemies.

Preview

The argument that follows comes in six chapters. Chapter 2 places the role of business in historical perspective. I start by looking at the *record* of economic progress over the past half-century, drawing on some of the statistical evidence that bears on it. I then turn – and this is more speculative – to the *sources* of that progress; and in particular, I consider ways in which, and the extent to which, the substantial advances in material welfare that have been made, in many different countries across the world, can be linked to the activities of business enterprises. I argue that the link has been close and direct. This is not because it is a conscious aim of individual businesses to further economic progress: the link exists because, and in so far as, they are subject to the combination of opportunities and pressures that a market economy creates.

In this model, or vision, of the process of economic change, *the primary role of businesses, as seen from outside rather than from the perspective of individual firms, is to act as agents of economic progress.* My argument points to a conditionally positive conclusion, namely, that there is good reason to take a favourable view of the past, present and potential future contribution of business enterprises to the general welfare, provided – and this is the 'conditional' part – they are operating in competitive market-directed economies and situations. In so far as that condition is met today, there is no apparent need to redefine the role and purposes of individual businesses in order to ensure that they continue to act in ways that will broadly promote the material welfare of people in general. What *is* chiefly required, now as in the past, is the preservation, extension and reinforcement of a well-functioning market economy. This will both enable and induce businesses to carry out their primary role.

The advocates of CSR take a different view. Some of them might question my treatment of the past, on the grounds that it paints too rosy a picture of economic history and of the benefits that a market economy gives rise to. They might also argue that it glosses over environmental problems and threats which can be seen as arising from economic growth. But the main single source of disagreement between us is that they believe that the world has been transformed, over the past ten to twenty years, in ways that call for a new and wider conception of business responsibilities.

Such a transformation could occur in either or both of two different ways. On the one hand, it could result from changes in the objective situation, through actual developments on the world economic scene. On the other hand, it could also arise from changes in ideas, perceptions and attitudes, in how people view the world and the role of businesses within it. Although of course the two influences are connected, it is convenient to look at them separately.

In Chapter 3 the focus is on the objective situation. Those who favour CSR typically argue that the world economy, and with it the problems and responsibilities of business, have been fundamentally changed by *'globalisation'*. The chapter sets out reasons for questioning or rejecting this interpretation of events, drawing in part on what is said in *Misguided Virtue* and in a subsequent article of mine on the role and status of the World Trade Organization (WTO).[6] I argue that recent globalisation has had neither the properties nor the effects ascribed to it. Seen in true perspective, the changes that it has brought have confirmed rather than put in question the already established primary role of business.

The support for CSR, and the pressures on companies to endorse and give effect to it, have indeed arisen from recent changes on the world scene. But the decisive changes have been, not in the objective situation, but rather in the general climate of opinion relating to it. This evolution of thinking and attitudes is reviewed in Chapter 4. It can be seen as a development, and a reinforcement, of ideas which can be grouped under the heading of *global salvationism*. These ideas, and the view of the world that underlies them, are not new, nor are they well founded; but they have recently gained ground for reasons which I outline. One reason is the emergence, and now widespread acceptance, of the notion of sustainable development as an objective and a guiding principle for governments and society.

As one result of this trend in the climate of opinion, CSR has caught on. It is now officially favoured by many governments, as also by various strands of public opinion both within the business world and outside it, largely because it is seen as giving expression to the notion of sustainable development. Hence there are

---

6   David Henderson, 'WTO 2002: imaginary crisis, real problems', *World Trade Review*, 1(3), 2002.

strong pressures on businesses, from many sources, to redefine their role, aims and conduct. The ways of thinking that give rise to these pressures pay little or no regard, however, to the primary role of business.

In Chapter 5, the focus is on individual business enterprises and the ways in which they are perceived, rather than on world events. I consider the role of profitability, and the issue of business motivation and responsibilities, in a modern market economy. Two questions that arise are, first, how to view and measure an enterprise's contribution to the welfare of people in general, and second, what can be done, whether by businesses themselves or by governments, to improve that contribution. I contrast two ways of responding to these questions. One is an economic approach, in which profitability is taken as a useful first-approximation indicator of the enterprise contribution, and a leading task of governments is to improve it as such, in particular by actions to ensure that profits are performance-related. From this standpoint there is no reason to question the pursuit of profits by enterprises, or to call for new forms of business motivation. A rival approach is now offered by the doctrine of CSR. This prescribes sustainable development as the goal for businesses today, with improved profitability as a happy outcome rather than a primary goal or criterion. I argue that this second approach does not stand or fall by the distorted view of globalisation that normally goes with it: the doctrine can be stated in a modified and less vulnerable form. Even then, however, it makes highly questionable assumptions, while its general adoption would weaken business performance of the primary role and hence reduce welfare. The more traditional economic approach, which focuses on the role of profits, provides a better guide to thought and action.

The idea that business profitability can be closely linked to the general welfare is not widely accepted, and in the latter part of Chapter 5 I consider the reasons for this. I comment on the uses of self-interest, issues of business morality and motivation, and the question of how closely the business contribution to the general welfare is linked to virtuous conduct and to concerns that go beyond individual self-interest and enterprise profitability. I argue that the doctrine of CSR reflects traditional over-preoccupation with motives and the resultant chronic though unwarranted suspicion of profits. It unthinkingly downgrades the primary role, and the claims to legitimacy and recognition, of profit-oriented private business. The more effective performance of the primary role depends, not on changing the aims, motives and strategies of businesses, but on actions which fall outside their competence. These are matters of public policy, not of enterprise conduct.

This particular aspect of economic policy forms the main subject of Chapter 6. I focus on one key element, namely, actions designed to increase the extent of economic freedom – in other words, the *liberalisation* of economic systems today. Contrary to what is often argued or assumed, there is everywhere, though more conspicuously in developing and transition countries than in more advanced economies, wide scope for action on these lines: it is not the case for any country, still less for the world in general, that in recent years governments around the world have carried 'neo-liberal' policies to extremes. I sketch out the principal ways in which liberalisation could now be taken further, through enlarging economic freedom and extending the scope of competitive markets.

Of course, economic policy has other aspects, and other objectives, than promoting the material welfare of people in general: in particular, governments and public opinion are deeply concerned with issues of fairness and equality. Clearly, there are possibilities of conflict here, between economic freedom and greater equality. However, I give reasons for thinking that the case for liberalisation today is not necessarily undermined, if considerations of fairness and equality are given weight. In the final section of this chapter I question further the claim of CSR adherents that businesses have now acquired the power, and with it the responsibility, to bring about a new and improved form of capitalism.

Finally, I review in Chapter 7 the changing fortunes of capitalism and the market economy over the whole period since the end of World War II, and consider the widely held but questionable view that capitalism has finally triumphed over socialism and is now free from serious challenge. I argue that the future of capitalism is more assured than that of the market economy, which has by no means won the day. The main issue now is not that of capitalism versus socialism, but rather the extent to which economies which can be described as capitalist are subject to collectivist influences and tendencies. In this connection, I outline the various anti-market forces and influences of today. These can be grouped together under the heading of *new millennium collectivism*. They chiefly comprise, first, the pressures constantly brought to bear by special interest groups for various forms of public concessions or support, and second, a range of anti-market beliefs and presumptions in which global salvationism is combined with the many forms of pre-economic thinking, mainly long established but with some recent additions, which I place under the heading of 'do-it-yourself economics' (DIYE).

As in the past, economic policies, and trends in policy, will probably continue to feature both liberal and interventionist elements. It is not certain that the latter will prevail on balance, and they are in any case unlikely to pose a threat to capitalism as such. But the choice between different variants of capitalism, some more collectivised than others, is a real one. Today's collectivist influences and tendencies could limit economic freedom further, in ways that would affect, not just consumption of material goods and services, but the quality of life in general.

2 ECONOMIC PROGRESS AND THE ROLE OF BUSINESS

The record of progress

As to the past record of economic progress, I draw on a recently published study by the leading authority, Angus Maddison.[1] In it he presents comprehensive estimates, for all the countries and regions of the world and as far back as he considers feasible, of population, output (GDP), and GDP per head. I take these latter figures, of GDP per head, as indicators of economic progress. Historically, rising GDP per head has gone together with longer life expectation, advances in health, higher educational standards, some notable environmental improvements, and greater leisure; and it can reasonably be taken as a first-approximation measure of material welfare.[2]

Maddison's figures for GDP and GDP per head are given in a common unit of measurement of his own devising, namely, 1990 international US dollars: he corrects both for price level *changes* over time and for price level *differences* between countries. I use

---

1   Angus Maddison, *The World Economy: Historical Statistics*, OECD Development Centre, Paris, 2003.
2   It is sometimes argued that as an indicator of welfare GDP per head yields values that are too high, given that deductions have to be made to turn it into an index of 'sustainable welfare'. This view is contested, in the context of recent British figures, by Nicholas Crafts in 'UK Real National Income, 1950–98: Some Grounds for Optimism', *National Institute Economic Review*, 181, July 2002.

comparative figures of GDP per head, all taken from this recent study and expressed in these common international units, to present a summary historical sketch of recent economic progress.

I begin with Australia in the middle of the twentieth century. In Maddison's tables, Australia appears for the year 1950 as the fourth-richest country in the world, with only the USA, Switzerland and New Zealand placed above it. The 1950 figure for its GDP per head, rounded off, is $7,400. Judged in relation both to its own past and the record of other countries, Australia already had at that time, in the mid-twentieth century, a well-established claim to be viewed as an economic success story.

Suppose that we imagine ourselves as back in the early 1950s, peering then into the ever-clouded economic future, but with the benefit of Maddison's present-day estimates for changes over the years up to 1950. From the perspective of mid-century, what would have been a reasonable expectation as to Australian GDP per head by the century's end?

Any such projection would have had to start from the growth record of the past. From Maddison's latest estimates, the annual average rate of growth of GDP per head in Australia over the 80 years from 1870 to 1950 appears as close to 1 per cent, with little difference between the first half of the period, up to World War I, and the second half.[3] A continuation of this growth rate for the period 1950–2000 would have brought an increase in GDP per head of close to 65 per cent, with a figure for the year 2000 of some $12,000. A more sanguine assessment might have foreseen an acceleration of the growth rate, with an average of perhaps 1.5

3   Less recent estimates had shown a rather higher rate of growth for 1870–1913 than for 1913–50.

per cent per annum for the second half of the century; and this would have implied rather more than a doubling of Australian GDP per head, with a figure of $15,000–16,000 for the year 2000.

Although in the early 1950s such a predicted increase could well have been viewed as close to an upper limit of the probable, the actual outcome for the half-century was much better. Maddison's figure for GDP per head in Australia in 2000, as given in this new volume, is close to $21,500. This is almost triple the 1950 figure, while the annual average growth rate for 1950–2000 appears as approximately 2.1 per cent. By this test, therefore, Australian economic performance in the second half of the twentieth century greatly exceeded what it would have been reasonable to expect before the event. Judged by past standards, which themselves had been high by comparison with most other economies, and which had made Australia one of the richest countries in the world, that performance appears as truly remarkable.

Was Australia exceptional in this? Not at all. To the contrary, its relative position in the world had slipped by 2000 (that of New Zealand, by the way, had slipped much farther); and almost without exception, GDP per head in the economies which like Australia were already well advanced in 1950 had grown since then at average rates which were comparable with, or higher than, the notably high rate which was realised in Australia. For all these countries – in western Europe, North America, Australasia and Japan – and taking the second half of the twentieth century as a whole, this has been a period in which material welfare has advanced at rates substantially higher than past history would have suggested as likely or even possible. So far as I know, no one predicted this.

But the record of economic progress during this half-century goes beyond the group of already advanced countries, in ways that no one foresaw or even imagined, and which mark an even more decisive break with the past. Up to 1950, and even for some years after, it was possible to question whether modern economic growth, and with it a sustained rise in material welfare for people in general, could be achieved outside a restricted group, a 'magic circle', of countries which were all, with the exception of Japan, either European or of predominantly European origin.[4] Despite the progress made from the later nineteenth century onwards in a number of poorer countries, especially though not only in Latin America, such doubts could still be held. They have now been wholly dispelled. In the course of these five decades, an increasing number of initially poorer countries, some of them very poor, achieved rates of growth in material standards of living which were either rare or wholly unprecedented anywhere in earlier history. It has been conclusively shown that modern economic growth is not the monopoly of a magic circle of favoured countries.

Which are these newly successful countries? On Maddison's evidence, and leaving aside the smallest economies with a population in 2000 of less than 1 million, there are some 25–30 countries at least which have good claims to be included in the list. Among these, the leaders are the fifteen countries outside the magic circle in which GDP per head increased more than fivefold – in some cases much more – between 1950 and 2000. In this remarkable group there are four European economies – Greece, Ireland,

---

4   I take this magic circle to comprise nineteen countries. Of these, fourteen are European – the fifteen pre-enlargement members of the European Union less Greece, Ireland, Portugal and Spain, together with Iceland, Norway and Switzerland. The other five countries are the USA, Canada, Australia, New Zealand and Japan.

Portugal, and Spain. All of these except Ireland were classed as developing countries until well into the period, while Ireland was widely perceived as a borderline case. Seven of the remaining countries are in East Asia: these comprise the four star performers which are Hong Kong, South Korea, Singapore and Taiwan, together with Malaysia, Thailand, and China where the record of truly outstanding economic progress begins with the economic reforms of 1978. There are two countries from West Asia, Israel and Oman.[5] In Latin America, there is only Puerto Rico; and in Africa, Botswana (where in 2000 the full impact of Aids was still to be felt). By the end of the century, GDP per head in ten of these countries – the four in Europe, the four East Asian stars, and Israel and Puerto Rico – was far above the figure of close to $10,000 that the USA had achieved by 1950, while Hong Kong, Singapore and Ireland had all advanced beyond $20,000.

Three other developing countries where the $10,000 mark had been passed by the year 2000 are two small island economies, Mauritius and Trinidad, and Chile, where the growth rate of GDP per head was over 3 per cent per annum for the last quarter of the century. Countries which were considerably poorer than these in 1950, but where over the next half-century GDP per head rose more than fourfold, are Lesotho, Tunisia and Turkey, with Indonesia and Swaziland not far behind. Three Asian countries besides those already listed in which growth rates have been notably high for the period 1980–2000 are India and Sri Lanka, following moderate growth over the previous 30 years, and Vietnam, where

---

5   Alongside Israel, the West Bank and Gaza could also be included on the basis of a comparison between 1950 and 2000. Maddison surmises, however, that between 2000 and 2002 the GDP per head of these territories may have fallen by some 40 per cent.

not surprisingly GDP per head was not much higher in 1980 than in 1950. Moving down the list, there are a further dozen or so developing countries where for the period 1950–2000 as a whole the annual average growth rate exceeded 2 per cent. Half a century ago this would have been viewed as a remarkably high figure for any economy over such a length of time.

Varying fortunes

To be sure, these success stories are only part of the picture. As was to be expected, there have been large differences in economic performance over this half-century, both as between different periods of time, within countries and regions of the world, and, still more, as between different countries and regions. The most conspicuous differences have been those between the more successful and the less successful developing countries. Over the 50-year period as a whole the countries of Asia (excluding Japan, as a magic circle member) have done much better than those of Africa: in 1950 the average figure for GDP per head for these Asian countries, taken together, was some 30 per cent below that for the African continent, whereas by 2000 it was well over twice as high. The gap in performance between the more dynamic Asian developing economies and their counterparts, in Latin America and the rest of Asia as well as in Africa, widened conspicuously in the last two decades of the century. Over this latter period there were fourteen developing economies in East and South Asia in which GDP per head increased by more than 50 per cent. The combined population of these fourteen countries in 2000 was over 3 billion – just over half the population of the world. Their combined GDP per head rose by a factor of just over two and a half, with an average annual rate of growth of over 4 per cent. Within the group, there were nine conspicuously successful economies in which GDP per head more than doubled over the two decades: besides China and the four East Asian stars, this latter sub-group comprised India, Malaysia, Thailand and Vietnam.[6] By contrast, GDP per head for the African continent was nearly 5 per cent *lower* in 2000 than in 1980, while for Latin America there was an increase of only 8 per cent between the two years.

It is not only in Africa and Latin America that generally high growth rates for the period 1950–80 have not been sustained since then: there has been a falling away in economic performance in recent years in most of the transition countries of eastern Europe and the former USSR. On Maddison's figures, GDP per head in 2000 for the countries that made up the USSR was some 37 per cent below that for 1990. In his outstanding survey of world economic history, *The World Economy: A Millennial Perspective* (already quoted above, on the half-title verso), Maddison identifies, on the basis of performance since 1973, a category which he labels as 'faltering economies'. The list comprises all the countries of Latin America and Africa, all the transition economies, and 40 out of 56 countries in Asia: in total, it extends to 168 countries, containing some 35 per cent of the world population. He writes of them (p. 129) that: '... deterioration in economic performance since the golden age [i.e. since 1973] has been alarming. In the successor states of the former USSR, it has been catastrophic'.

In my view, this is too dark a picture. The list of 168 includes

---

6   The other five countries in the list of fourteen are Bangladesh, Indonesia, Myanmar (Burma), Pakistan and Sri Lanka. The International Monetary Fund (IMF) now classes Hong Kong, Singapore, South Korea and Taiwan, along with the core OECD countries and Israel, in its category of 'advanced economies'.

56 small economies with a total population of only 20 million in 2000, some of which have not in fact been faltering. Of the remaining 112 countries, there are 25 or so where past or current economic performance, or both, can be viewed as reasonably good: some of them are to be found among the success stories referred to above. Their combined population in 2000 comes to not far short of 500 million. Further, the past few years have brought rapid progress in some of the remaining countries that Maddison refers to: in particular, the average GDP per head of the group of fifteen countries that made up the former USSR is estimated by the staff of the IMF to have increased by 21 per cent between 2000 and 2003.[7]

It is true that, even with these various subtractions and reservations, the list of falterers remains long, while many though by no means all of its members are among the poorest countries in the world. The relative gap between GDP per head in these latter countries and that in the advanced economies has widened significantly; and in this respect, economic inequality in the world has increased. But despite the recent falling away of economic performance in many countries, and the persistence of low levels of income per head in most though not all of these, it remains true that for most of the world the period from 1950 to 2000, judged by all past standards, emerges as one of striking economic progress. Over the half-century world output per head, on Maddison's showing, increased by a factor of 2.85, with an annual average rate of growth of 2.1 per cent: this compares with an increase of just over two-thirds from 1900 to 1950, with a growth rate of only 1 per

---

7   International Monetary Fund, *World Economic Outlook*, Washington, DC, April 2004, p. 193.

cent per annum. For the developing countries of Latin America, Asia and Africa, the relative improvement, as between the two periods, was greater: their combined average GDP per head rose by just under one third only in the first half of the century, while in the second half it increased by a factor of 2.75. In a number of cases, mostly in Asia, the growth rates of newly emergent economies actually exceeded those that were typically reached within the magic circle, which themselves were substantially higher than in any previous half-century. It is this spread of modern and accelerated economic growth to a far wider range of countries than ever before, including the two most populous countries in the world, which is the most notable feature of the period as a whole.

Obscuring the record of progress

This record of unforeseen economic achievement often goes unrecognised or undervalued. One reason for such a misreading of the past is a preoccupation with particular inter-country differences with respect to both GDP per head and its growth over time. For example, the authors of *Walking the Talk* assert (p. 242) that 'we are far from achieving intragenerational equity', because 'we are faced with a growing gulf between rich and poor' in the world. This is doubly misleading.

First, the unqualified reference to 'a growing gulf' is not true of rich and poor countries in general, as distinct from those poor countries in which the growth of output per head has been slow or even negative. The statement takes no account of the fact that, in the course of the past half-century or so, the numerous citizens of the more economically successful poorer countries have been rapidly catching up with their counterparts in the former magic circle. The following can serve as illustrations:

- In 1950 the GDP per head of Australia was over three times that of Hong Kong. By the year 2000, after a period when, as noted,the rate of growth in Australian GDP per head was substantially higher than ever before, the two figures were virtually identical.
- In 1950 the GDP per head in Taiwan was just above one eighth of that in the UK, while for 2000 the ratio was seven-eighths.
- In 1978, when the first decisive steps towards economic reform were taken in China, the ratio of US to Chinese GDP per head was nearly 19 to 1. By the year 2000 it had fallen almost to 8 to 1.
- Between 1980 and 2000, the combined GDP per head of the nine most strikingly successful Asian developing economies listed above, which had a combined population in 2000 of just over 2.5 billion, increased by 170 per cent. The corresponding figure for the core OECD countries taken together, with a total population in 2000 of just over 850 million, was 50 per cent only.[8]
- Taking the period 1950–2000 as a whole, average GDP per head in the countries which initially were the poorest, all of them with a 1950 figure of less than $800, increased by a factor of over four and a half, which was not only

---

8 I use the term 'core OECD countries' to refer to the 24 states that were members of the organisation from the early 1970s to the 1990s when the membership was expanded, less Turkey, which was considerably poorer than the rest. The group comprises the nineteen 'magic circle' countries plus Greece, Ireland, Portugal and Spain.

unprecedentedly high but higher than that for the magic circle countries.

The substantial relative gains thus made by some developing countries, and by one half or more of the world's population, are the more remarkable in that, as seen already, output per head in the magic circle economies was itself growing over these periods of comparison at historically high rates.

It is true that the gap between the richest and the poorest countries in the world has widened in recent years, but this is only part of the picture. A balanced assessment of what has happened to poor countries and poor people has to extend to the world as a whole, and to take account of the success stories and intermediate cases among the developing countries as well as the falterers. In doing so, it must also take account of differences in population, rather than treating developing countries large and small as equivalent units.

Second, *it is wrong to think either of cross-country inequalities, or of differences in growth rates which serve to 'widen the gap', as evidence of 'inequity'.* Let me take a specific case to illustrate the general point, by comparing developments in Nigeria and South Korea in recent decades. For 1950, Maddison now puts the GDP per head of both countries at very much the same level which was little more than one-third of the average figure for the world as a whole in that year. Between 1950 and 2000 the Nigerian figure is shown as having increased by about 50 per cent, as compared with a three-fold increase for the world as a whole: by 2000, Nigerian GDP per head stood at less than one-fifth of the world average. By contrast, GDP per head in South Korea for the year 2000 was almost 20 times the level of the early 1950s, and well over twice the world average. It is clear that over the half-century there has indeed been a 'growing gulf' between these two economies. But such a development does not constitute 'inequity'. The fact that Nigeria's economic perform-ance has outclassed that of South Korea is neither a result nor a manifestation of injustice, nor would the cause of 'intragen-erational equity' – or the interests of Nigerians – have been well served if growth in South Korea had been slower, whether by accident or design. It is better to view the economic progress made by countries in general, and poor countries in particular, as a positive gain for the world, rather than to label it as a problem, or a source of inequity, on no stronger grounds than that it has not been equally matched by others.

It is true that over the half-century as a whole GDP per head has grown faster in the core OECD countries taken together than in almost all countries in Africa, the great majority of countries in Latin America, and many developing countries in Asia. It is also true that, despite the fact that OECD growth rates have been much lower since 1973 than in the previous quarter of a century, they have none the less exceeded those of the many faltering econ-omies over the period 1980–2000. But it is not the 'widening gap' between these richer economies and the less successful poorer ones which poses a problem, but the slow rate of progress in the latter. The present situation of the faltering economies is not the result of continuing economic progress on the part of rich coun-tries, nor would it be improved if the growth rates of the latter fell away to such an extent that the gap was narrowed. To concentrate attention on the gap is a mistake.[9]

---

9   This is true not only in relation to measures of real income per head, but also for other indicators of welfare. Life expectancy is one example. According to UN

A number of recent studies have reviewed one or both of two much-debated questions: first, how far recent growth in output per head in developing countries has brought with it a reduction in the total numbers of those living in poverty; and second, whether or not the distribution of income in the world as a whole, allowing for changes within countries as well as between them, has become more equal.[10] Different answers can be given, chiefly because of differing views as to (1) the appropriate period of comparison, (2) how poverty is to be defined, (3) how inequality is best measured, and (4) the weight to be given to the various data sources relating to the level and distribution of national income and expenditure, including household surveys. There is wide agreement, however, first, that hundreds of millions of people have been raised above the poverty lines that are mainly used, and second, that inequality between individuals across the world as a whole has probably fallen. One summary of the evidence that seems near the mark was provided two years ago in an international conference by a

estimates (*World Population Prospects: the 2002 Revision*), average life expectancy in 'less developed countries' rose from 41 years in 1950–55 to 66 years in 2000–05. The corresponding figures for 'more developed countries' were 63 years and 76 years. Thus the gap between the two groups of countries was more than halved, from 22 years to 10 years. But the world would not now be a better place, even though the gap would be substantially narrower, if life expectancy in the 'more developed' countries had increased only to 70 years over the period.

10 These studies include in particular: Surjit S. Bhalla, *Imagine There's No Country: Poverty, Inequality and Growth in the Era of Globalization* (Institute of International Economics, Washington, DC, 2003); Xavier Sala-i-Martin, *The Disturbing 'Rise' of Global Income Inequality*, NBER Working Paper 8904, Cambridge, MA, 2002; and David Dollar and Aart Kraay, 'Spreading the Wealth', *Foreign Affairs*, 81(1), 2002. A recent article in *The Economist* (13 March 2004, pp. 83–5) provides a helpful brief guide to the evidence and the current debate, and a fuller review is contained in Chapter 9 of Martin Wolf's outstanding new book, *Why Globalization Works: The Case for the Global Market Economy*, Yale University Press, New Haven, CT, and London, 2004.

Turkish Treasury official, Melih Nemli. He argued that: 'As long as we agree that we should use purchasing power parity, weight countries by population and ... include China and India in the analysis, the empirical evidence, despite all the data problems, is overwhelming that poverty rates and the poverty headcount have declined ... and that world inequality has fallen over the past two decades...'[11]

In any case, whatever may be the most convincing estimates of these trends, the main aspect to stress, which remains unaffected, is the record of economic success in this past half-century. It is the high rates of growth of output per head in developing countries, chiefly though not only in Asia, which have, first, made possible the notable reductions in poverty that have occurred, and second, offset what would otherwise have been a trend towards greater inequality across the world as the core OECD countries continued to advance.

The moral of the story

Looking back over this half-century, as indeed over a longer historical period, three features of all the leading economic success stories, in richer and poorer countries alike, stand out:

- Generally speaking, the sustained high growth rates owed little or nothing to direct foreign assistance.[12] They were not

---

11 The quotation is from David Gruen, Terry O'Brien and Jenny Lawson, *Globalisation, Living Standards and Inequality: Recent Progress and Continuing Challenges*, Reserve Bank of Australia, 2002, p.255. This volume contains the proceedings of a conference held in Sydney in May 2002, the text of which is available on the website of the Reserve Bank of Australia.

12 Israel may be one exception to this generalisation.

the outcome of official aid programmes, whether bilateral or multilateral, of public-spirited conduct by large international firms, or of collective resolutions and initiatives on the part of 'the international community'.

- These developments have further confirmed what earlier economic history already indicated clearly, that everywhere the material progress of people, rich and poor alike, depends primarily on the dynamism of the economies in which they live and work. The progress of workers does not chiefly depend on the activities of trade unions or the regulation of wages and employment, which may indeed make economies less dynamic; and advances made by poor people through the development of social services and progressive taxation can be overshadowed by the gains which arise from economic growth.[13] Again, there is no basis for the widely held belief that the gains from higher GDP accrue in the first place largely or entirely to the rich, so that poor people, in the absence of collective provision for them, are dependent for improvements in their lot on a process of 'trickle down' that cannot be relied on. This metaphor has no place in serious discussion.

- The success stories confirm that, in economies where a number of background conditions are broadly met and maintained, material progress is now likely to go ahead at rates which in my days as a recently graduated teacher of

13   In *Walking the Talk*, the authors rightly make the point (p. 40) that 'Countries do not have low incidences of poverty because of their welfare programs but largely because they have created frameworks that encourage business enterprise'. But this is not a leading theme or message of the book. In any case, for reasons set out in the remaining sections of this chapter, 'encouragement' of business is not the point.

economics, over half a century ago, would have been viewed as inconceivable. These background conditions are that there is reasonably stable government, with no serious internal disorders, that governments act responsibly in matters of public finance and the control of the money supply, that property rights are well established and maintained, that economic decision-making rests largely with private individuals and enterprises, and that the economy is substantially open to transactions with the rest of the world. These are in fact the main conditions, political as well as economic, which make it possible for a market economy to operate effectively. To realise them, and keep them in place, is no light or straightforward task.

The sources of progress

Even given these background conditions, a large question remains. How is one to account for the kind of economic dynamism which makes possible substantial and sustained advances in material welfare? What are the *sources* of economic progress, as distinct from the *conditions*? There are many ways of approaching this question, and many ways of answering it. Here is my own first-approximation one-sentence answer: *the primary direct impulse to economic progress comes from profit-related activities and initiatives on the part of business enterprises*. This is true of countries everywhere, past and present, and rich and poor alike.

Why should this be? Because a dynamic economy, in which rapid and sustained economic growth is taking place, is characterised by continuous change and innovation; and the array of changes and innovations which at any given time is proceeding within such an economy is largely the outcome of purposive activity by enterprises.

The economist who has expressed this idea most cogently and memorably is Joseph Schumpeter. In some brilliant early chapters of his book *Capitalism, Socialism and Democracy*, first published in 1942, Schumpeter outlines the essential features of capitalist evolution, which he characterises as a process of 'creative destruction'. He writes (p. 83): 'The fundamental impulse that sets and keeps the capitalist engine in motion comes from the new consumers' goods, the new methods of production or transportation, the new markets, the new forms of industrial organization that capitalist enterprise creates'.

In this view of the world, businesses are the main vehicles, the principal initiating agents, for the changes that bring with them, for the economy as a whole, rising productivity and higher material welfare. To be sure, this outcome is not what individual enterprises themselves consciously set out to achieve: their aims are, and have to be, more limited and specific (more on this below). All the same, this is the economy-wide result of the sum of their activities.

A different view of innovation and economic dynamism is of course possible, in which the part played by business enterprises is more reactive and incidental. According to this view, economic growth is principally a function of technical progress, which itself arises chiefly from advances in knowledge. These advances in turn result for the most part from research and development activity, much of which is sponsored by agencies other than corporations and may be neither profit-driven nor directly market-oriented. Granted that technical progress may often if not typically be brought into effect through the actions and decisions of business enterprises, the underlying creative role, which lays the ground for these innovative commercially based activities, is seen as being played by persons and institutions that are for the most part outside, and separated from, the business world.

This alternative vision of economic evolution is explicitly considered, and rejected, by Schumpeter. He writes (p. 110):

> Was not the observed performance due to that stream of inventions that revolutionized the technique of production rather than to the businessman's hunt for profits? The answer is in the negative. The carrying into effect of these technological novelties was of the essence of that hunt ... It is ... quite wrong to say, as so many economists do, that capitalist enterprise was one, and technological progress a second, distinct factor in the observed development of output; they were essentially one and the same thing or, as we may put it, the former was the propelling force of the latter.

He thus views scientific and technical advances as *endogenous* – as forming an integral part of a business-led process of economic change, rather than acting as an external (or exogenous) influence on it.

I would like to cite briefly, in chronological order, three expert witnesses in broad support of Schumpeter's thesis. First is the late Jacob Schmookler, in a remarkable book entitled *Invention and Economic Growth*.[14] Two quotations will give the flavour of the book's main argument: '... invention is largely an economic activity which, like other economic activities, is pursued for gain'

---

14   Jacob Schmookler, *Invention and Economic Growth*, Harvard University Press, Cambridge, MA, 1966.

(p. 206); and '... inventions are usually made because men want to solve economic problems or capitalize on economic opportunities ...' (p. 207).

Schmookler's book is taken as a point of departure in Chapter 5 of Maurice Scott's likewise remarkable (and in my view surprisingly neglected) book, *A New View of Economic Growth*.[15] Scott argues (p. 131) that 'scientific discovery and invention are best regarded as forms of investment', and that, like other forms of investment, they are to be seen as responses to the economic opportunities that are continuously generated by investment expenditures in general.

More recently, Schumpeter's thesis was made the subject of a set of lectures given at the University of Graz by my third witness, Nathan Rosenberg, in a series to which Schumpeter's name is attached.[16] Although Rosenberg is critical of some aspects of Schumpeter's views on science, he believes that (p. 18) 'both science and technology have been rendered a great deal more endogenous in the course of the twentieth century', and he offers evidence in support of this view.

No doubt dissenting witnesses could also be called, who would question or qualify Schumpeter's strong statement as to the dependence of technical progress on profit-led business initiatives. It may be reasonable to think in terms of a spectrum of

---

15 Maurice FitzGerald Scott, *A New View of Economic Growth*, Oxford University Press, 1989. The argument of the book has been later summarised and restated by Scott, with particular reference to the sources of technical progress and advances of knowledge, in an article entitled 'A New Theory of Endogenous Growth', published in 1996 in the *Oxford Review of Economic Policy*, 8(4).

16 Nathan Rosenberg, *Schumpeter and the Endogeneity of Technology: Some American perspectives*, Routledge, London and New York, 2000. The book begins with an admirable survey of Schumpeter's thought and his place in the history of economics.

interrelated activities, from discovery through invention to inno-vation and application, where the influence of economic oppor-tunities on motives and choices increases as one moves across it. The fundamental point, however, is that technical progress is not to be viewed wholly or even largely as an independently given factor, rather than as an outcome of the working of a market-led economy.

I believe that the case for Schumpeter's view of these rela-tionships has been strengthened by the spread of modern economic growth to countries outside the former magic circle. It is chiefly in the rich countries, where businesses generally are already using advanced methods and techniques, that further gains in productivity are often closely linked to what current research and development can provide by way of discoveries and inventions. In less advanced economies, there are large potential gains still to be made from changes and initiatives which are not so dependent on further additions to the world's stock of knowledge: firms can draw on what is already known and proved. The astonishing economic progress of the four Asian stars, and more recently of China, has not resulted from successful activities, there or elsewhere, on the part of men in white coats in laboratories. These and other previously poor countries now account for a far higher proportion of the growth in world GDP than was the case in earlier periods.

Entrepreneurship, opportunity and competitive pressures

In Schumpeter's vision of the capitalist process, a leading innovative role is played by business *entrepreneurs*. Here is his description (p. 132) of what the role of the entrepreneur involves and requires:

> To act with confidence beyond the range of familiar beacons and to overcome ... resistance [to change] requires aptitudes that are present in only a small fraction of the population and that define the entrepreneurial type as well as the entrepreneurial function. This function does not essentially consist in either inventing anything or otherwise creating the conditions which the enterprise exploits. It consists in getting things done.

This description of the distinctive entrepreneurial role and skills is well illustrated by the career of Lang Hancock (as outlined in the Preface). In his case, special emphasis should be given to the aspect of overcoming resistance to change.

The main initial source of resistance that Hancock had to contend with was the Australian Commonwealth government, through its prohibition, introduced in 1938, of the export of iron ore from Australia. This prohibition has been described by a former Western Australian business leader, Charles Copeman – justly, I think – as 'an early example of government-imposed sustainable development policy', and the story of it has been well told by a leading Australian historian, Geoffrey Blainey.[17] It was only with the removal of the export ban – for which Hancock had campaigned strongly – that the way was opened for large-scale and innovative mining operations in the Pilbara. At state level, a further obstacle to these operations was the prohibition by the government of Western Australia of the pegging of claims

---

17   In an article entitled 'The Cargo Cult in Mineral Policy', *Economic Record*, December 1968.

by private agents to exploration rights for iron ore deposits. This prohibition was also lifted.

There is nothing unusual in such a story: economic history offers many instances in which the scope for enterprises to undertake worthwhile investments has been restricted by government prohibitions or regulations, the removal of which has opened up new vistas. Nor are such instances difficult to find today, as will be seen in Chapter 6 below.

A notable recent case of decontrol is that of China following the decisive turning point of 1978. In another book of his, Angus Maddison lists three main factors as having contributed to 'the greater efficiency and higher productivity growth of the Chinese economy':[18]

- First, 'peasants regained control and management of their land'.
- Second, 'there was a huge expansion of small-scale industry, particularly in rural areas'.
- Third, 'the rigid monopoly of foreign trade, and the policy of autarchic self-reliance were abandoned'.

Under all these headings, new possibilities were opened up by the removal or relaxation of official prohibitions, regulations and controls. The measures that Maddison lists formed the core of a programme of reforms which greatly extended the scope for market-directed activities and transactions. His summary of events, as quoted on page 22 above, is that 'since 1978, Chinese performance has been transformed by liberalisation of the economy' (*The World Economy: A Millennial Perspective*, p. 146).

---

18   Angus Maddison, *Chinese Economic Performance in the Long Run*, OECD Development Centre, Paris, 1999, p. 16.

This recasting of economic policies has cleared the way for a host of Chinese business enterprises to grasp opportunities and introduce innovations.

A point to note is that the enterprises which have sprung up in, and contributed to, this recent growth process in China have come in all shapes and sizes, and many of them have been quite small. This illustrates a general truth. It is not just the big companies and the multinational corporations which can play the creative role that Schumpeter describes in promoting innovation. Within a market economy all business enterprises, small as well as large, may serve this function in some degree – even though it can be argued that only a minority of business leaders qualify for the description of 'entrepreneur'.

There is still an important missing element in the picture just sketched out of the business contribution to dynamic growth. I have spoken of the positive disposition of entrepreneurs within a market-directed economy, their readiness to identify, and to respond to, economic opportunities. But clearly there is another powerful motive and influence at work to promote innovation. Businesses large and small make investments, introduce changes, and engage in innovation, not only to exploit perceived opportunities, but also to ward off possible threats to their profitability and even their survival. This defensive motivation likewise helps to account for the impressive business-related growth performance of market economies, and it forms the theme of William Baumol's recently published book, *The Free-Market Innovation Machine*.[19] In

---

19   William J. Baumol, *The Free-Market Innovation Machine: Analyzing the growth miracle of capitalism* (Princeton University Press, Princeton, NJ, and Oxford, 2002). Baumol makes the point that 'large firms use innovation as a prime competitive weapon', and quotes Schumpeter on the opening page of the book.

his opening chapter (p. 3), Baumol says that his analysis 'attributes this [growth] performance primarily to competitive pressures, not present in other types of economy, that force firms in the relevant sectors of the economy to unrelenting investment in innovation and that ... provide incentives for the rapid dissemination and exchange of improved technology throughout the economy'.

This emphasis on competitive pressures is justified. The contribution of businesses to economic progress arises, not just from the creative scope that a market economy offers to enterprises and to entrepreneurial talents, but also from the intense and pervasive competition which it generates, and which itself typically arises from the ways in which other businesses are exploiting opportunities and possibilities for innovation. The two aspects, positive and defensive, are not separate, but interdependent and mutually reinforcing. They take effect through their impact on enterprise profitability.

Both aspects are strengthened in so far as international flows of trade and capital are made freer: business opportunities are opened up, as in the case of exports of iron ore from Australia, while competition is made keener in so far as restrictions on the entry of foreign goods, or on the establishment of foreign-owned enterprises, are dismantled or reduced. It is no accident that the historically high growth rates of output over this past half-century have been accompanied by an even faster expansion of international trade: in round terms, world output rose almost sevenfold between 1950 and 2000, while the volume of world trade increased by a factor of over 20. The story of economic progress over these decades is in part a story of external liberalisation – of the opening up of national economies to new possibilities for competition, innovation and advance.

To sum up under this heading, the opportunities for businesses to innovate, and the pressures on them to do so, are two sides of the same coin. Both give rise to economic advances, both are the product of economic freedom, including the freedom to engage in cross-border transactions, both are signalled by prospective enterprise profits, and both are defining features of a competitive market economy.

Because of these interrelated features, the role of business enterprises as vehicles of economic progress is linked, now as in the past, with 'capitalism', private ownership and profit-directed activity. Admittedly, GDP per head in the communist countries of central and eastern Europe and the former USSR appears to have risen fast over the period from 1950 to around the mid-1970s; but it has since become clear that socialist economic systems of this kind cannot function effectively in the world of today. As to more market-oriented economies, it is true that within them business enterprises can be publicly owned, and that public enterprises may themselves promote innovation and have regard to profitability. But public ownership typically goes together with restrictions on entry into the industries concerned and protection against imports, both of which greatly narrow the scope for competition. Further, public enterprises are normally secure against the threat of bankruptcy; and to a greater extent than their private counterparts, they are subject to forms of political direction and interference that are designed to limit the possibilities for change or to slow down the process of adjustment to it. All this tends to reduce both the pressures on their managers to act entrepreneurially and their scope for doing so. A fully competitive market economy, which serves to generate and maintain such pressures and opportunities, has to be one in which goods and services are typically provided by commercially oriented private firms.

The primary role of business

The above argument can be put in a single sentence. Past history, especially of the past half-century or so, offers clear evidence of rapid, sustained and increasingly widespread improvements in material welfare, and there is good reason to think that profit-oriented 'capitalist' business enterprises, operating within the framework of competitive market economies, have played, and are continuing to play, a large part in making such achievements possible. *From an economy-wide perspective, as distinct from that of the individual firm, this is the primary role of business.*

The effective performance of this role requires a framework of laws, institutions and political stability in which a market economy can function: the background conditions summarised above have to be established and maintained. Business itself may have a contribution to make under this heading, for, as Colin Robinson has noted in a recent essay: 'Rules are necessary if business life (as personal life) is to flourish, but they do not need to be set by government. For centuries rules of business life have evolved, being tested and filtered over time to produce robust norms of behaviour.'[20] All the same, the main responsibility for creating the necessary framework, which goes beyond norms and rules of conduct for enterprises, rests with governments rather then business. Further, it is for governments to decide how far,

---

20   Colin Robinson, 'From Nationalisation through Deregulation to Reregulation: The Changing Business Climate', in J. Hirst (ed.), *The Challenge of Change*, Profile, London, 2003.

and in what ways, to enlarge or restrict by law the market opportunities and competitive pressures that bear on both businesses and people in general. In doing so, they have to take account of other issues, and other aims of policy, than that of improving the performance of enterprises as a means to furthering economic progress: this latter aspect is taken up in Chapter 6 below.

The primary role of business, thus defined, is not one that individual enterprises consciously set out to play: it is not 'internalised', nor could it be. Within it, businesses are cast as agents of market-led change, but this is not because they have chosen to act as such. In any case, internalisation would serve little purpose, since the effective performance of the role does not depend on it. No one would claim that past and current material progress, as for example in the notable economic success stories referred to above, has resulted from a conscious commitment by enterprises to achieving such an outcome. The advances that capitalism has brought did not arise from the resolve of business leaders to make them possible, but from the operation of competitive market economies.

The primary role of business, then, is defined here without reference to either the objectives of enterprises or the motives of those who own, manage and direct them; and *its effective performance does not depend on a conscious attempt by business leaders to make the world a better place*. It derives its legitimacy, and its significance, from its bearing on the welfare of people in general. From this economy-wide standpoint, the role of businesses is instrumental, and the function of profits is to enable it to be performed. The interconnections between enterprise objectives and motivation and business performance of the primary role are explored in Chapter 5 below.

Why should this well-established constructive role not extend into the future? What is to prevent businesses from continuing to act as agents of economic progress – all the more so if the scope for them to do so is broadened, as it could well be if governments acted to bring this about, by further privatisation, further extension of market-based transactions, and further freeing of international trade and capital flows? Given the past record of capitalist achievement, why is it so widely held, in particular by the advocates of CSR, that businesses should now adopt a radically new model of corporate behaviour? Why is there so much social pressure on businesses today, from all sides including from within corporations themselves, to reform their outlook and conduct, and to broaden their objectives, in ways that give explicit weight to considerations of public welfare?

For many of today's radical reformers, the answer to these questions is clear. They believe that a new era has dawned. They argue that recent changes on the world scene have created dramatically new problems and opportunities, and that businesses have to redefine their role in order to play their full part in responding to these and, in so doing, to fulfil what have now become their social responsibilities. The next chapter presents a critique of this view, focusing chiefly on what are said to be the effects of 'globalisation'.

3 GLOBALISATION, 'CIVIL SOCIETY' AND 'GLOBAL GOVERNANCE'[1]

Caricaturing globalisation

In arguing that the world has been transformed, CSR advocates, along with many other people, point to *globalisation* as the main single underlying influence, the primary reason why the role of business now has to be rethought. This is the view taken by the authors of *Walking the Talk*, who write (p. 106) that: 'With increasing market globalization during the 1990s it became clear that business had a broader social responsibility or citizenship role'. On the dust jacket of the book, the question is posed: 'As planetary anxieties about globalization, poverty and climate change grow, where does the international business community stand?' *Walking the Talk* offers an answer to the question of where it *should* stand: CSR is presented as primarily a response to the challenges posed to international business by globalisation. To be sure, these are not the only perceived challenges: a second leading area of concern is with what are seen as current and prospective environmental problems and threats. But while these latter are

---

1 Globalisation is a large and highly topical subject, and a vast amount has been written on it. It is surveyed in two major recent studies: Martin Wolf's *Why Globalization Works*, already referred to above, and Jagdish Bhagwati's *In Defence of Globalisation*, Oxford University Press, 2004. Both these books cover the subject as a whole, while here I consider only those aspects of it that bear particularly on the role of business.

likewise thought of as calling for responses by business, they are not for the most part portrayed as dramatically new, in the sense that the globalisation of the last ten to fifteen years is taken to be.

What is meant by 'globalisation' here? I think the authors of the book, and CSR advocates generally, are using the term in its usual economic sense, to refer to a process of closer international economic integration. In such a process, the economic significance of distance, and still more of political boundaries, is diminished. Flows and transactions over long distances, and, especially, flows and transactions across frontiers, become a larger part of economic life. Developments of this kind have indeed been taking place in recent decades, and can be expected to continue: on balance, there has been a clear trend towards cross-border integration. So much is common ground.

However, the more recent moves towards closer economic integration, which have given rise to the term 'globalisation', are frequently misrepresented, both by advocates of CSR and by others. Globalisation is portrayed as a newly arisen economic tidal wave, which is sweeping hapless peoples and governments before it and creating, whether we like it or not, an anarchic borderless world. Three things are badly wrong with this picture.

First, it is unhistorical, since the trend towards closer international economic integration is not at all new. It was strongly in evidence over the century that ended in 1914; and though reversed in the period 1914–45, it was clearly re-established, albeit with many limitations, exceptions and local reversals, in the decades following World War II. It did not assume a new character, nor did it create a radically new situation, in the course of the 1990s.

Second, a borderless world does not now exist, nor is it even remotely in prospect. Although the various measures taken to liberalise trade and capital flows over the past 20 to 25 years have indeed been far-reaching, substantial and well-entrenched restrictions on these flows are still in place, while international migration remains strictly controlled. Liberalisation has by no means brought a fully integrated world economy, nor is the creation of such an economy advocated by any existing government.

Third, globalisation has not been forced on reluctant governments which had little choice but to accept it. To the contrary, the story of closer international economic integration, in recent years as in the past, is predominantly one of actions deliberately undertaken by the governments of national sovereign states. Governments have made trade and capital flows freer, and some of them have even made international migration flows freer, because they considered, with good reason, that this was in the interest of their peoples.

Alongside these mistaken general beliefs about globalisation, there are two further misconceptions relating to it which typically enter into the thinking of CSR supporters along with others. The widespread acceptance of these twin notions helps to explain not only the social pressures that are now brought to bear on businesses to turn a radically new leaf, but also the positive response to those pressures on the part of many elements in the business world.

The myth of 'marginalisation'

A belief that is now widely held, in the business world as well as more generally, is that globalisation has 'marginalised' poor countries. Hence – it is argued – there is a need to ensure that globalisation, and capitalism too, are 'given a human face'. Businesses are urged to help in this process, and contribute in new and more effective ways to the development of poor countries, by embracing 'global corporate citizenship'.

The charge of 'marginalisation', however, has no basis. It is true that, alongside the record of economic progress summarised in the previous chapter, and which closer international economic integration has helped to make possible, there is a dark side to the picture: as noted already, there is at present a long list, made up of both developing and transition countries, of economies that can be described as faltering. The various predicaments of these economies can, however, in no way be traced to globalisation, nor to harmful actions, failures or neglect on the part of international businesses. Generally speaking, these are the very countries in which, by contrast with the rest of the world, liberalisation, including liberalisation of trade and foreign investment flows, has not gone ahead. This partly accounts for their lack of progress, though other influences, varying in significance from case to case and often dominant, include climatic and ecological handicaps, wars, disease (especially since the onset of Aids), inadequate legal systems, civil disorder, and chronic misgovernment. One cannot blame globalisation in the world as a whole, nor liberalisation at home, for the deep-seated economic problems of Cuba under Castro, North Korea under Kim, Iran under the mullahs, Liberia and Somalia under their respective warlords, Nigeria under successive corrupt military dictatorships, Zimbabwe under Mugabe, Belarus under Lukashenko, Venezuela under Chávez, or Haiti under any of the governments that have held power there in recent decades. It is not globalisation which has 'marginalised' these and many other faltering economies, but rather internal factors, not least, in many cases, the actions and policies of their own governments.

By contrast, those developing and transition countries that have moved ahead have benefited from closer international economic integration in two ways. First, their governments have made their own trade and investment regimes freer: this has widened opportunities for business enterprises and increased the extent of competition, thus contributing to better economic performance. Second, the governments of the core OECD countries, broadly speaking, have maintained relatively liberal external trade regimes and taken trade liberalisation somewhat farther; and in doing so, as also through the continued expansion of their own economies, they have presided over growing market opportunities for goods and services produced in developing and transition countries. Under both these headings, economic policies favouring globalisation have contributed to making people in general in these latter groups of countries better off.

In this connection, the authors of *Walking the Talk* refer (p. 41) to 'the chronic lack of market access suffered by the world's poor', and (p. 52) to the risk of 'the developing world' being 'excluded from market opportunities'. Up to a point, these concerns are justified. The OECD countries generally, and in particular the USA and those of the EU, which are the ones that chiefly count as markets, continue to maintain well-established forms of selective protection – such as their agricultural support policies, quantitative restrictions on imports of textiles and clothing, and anti-dumping actions – which limit market access and are contrary to the interests of developing countries (as well as those of their own citizens). But here as elsewhere, the picture presented in the book is alarmist and misleading. There was and is no question of a general denial of market access on the part of OECD countries, while to use such language obscures the fact that the growth of exports from developing countries depends, not just on outside influences, but also on the actions of their own governments. Between 1973 and 1998 the estimated combined *volume* of exports from both China and Thailand rose by a factor of approximately 16, with a spectacular annual average rate of growth of close to 11 per cent. For Mexico, the corresponding ratio was almost 14. By contrast, exports from India over the same period increased in volume far less, though still considerably, by a factor of 4.2.[2] It is obvious from these figures that the products of developing countries were not at all denied access to OECD markets. It is also evident, from the historical record, that the main reason why Indian exports have not grown faster over the past half-century is to be found, not in the trade regimes of the OECD countries, but in the policies of restriction and protection pursued by the government of India. In China, by contrast, barriers to both imports and exports have been substantially reduced in recent years. One aspect of this far-reaching liberalisation of external trade is that China now has 'the lowest tariff protection of any developing country'.[3]

The myth of shifting power

A further serious misconception relates to the effects of globalisation on the distribution of power. Many advocates of CSR argue that corporations are now under an obligation to assume, if only by default, new and broader responsibilities on the international scene. To quote the authors of *Walking the Talk* (pp. 106–7): 'The

---

2   These numbers are derived from Table F-2 of Maddison, *The World Economy: A Millennial Perspective*, p. 361.

3   Nicholas R. Lardy, *Integrating China into the Global Economy*, Brookings Institution, Washington, DC, 2002, p. 9.

1990s … marked a radical rethink of the respective roles of the state and business in society … companies must be seen to be acting in keeping with their new powers and responsibilities'. It is now widely held, and endlessly reiterated on all sides, that globalisation, together with privatisation of state enterprises, has deprived national governments of their ability to determine policies and control events. This typically goes with a belief that the powers supposedly lost by governments have passed in large part to multinational enterprises (MNEs).

All too often, and inexcusably, evidence for this latter idea is offered in the form of figures comparing the turnover of big corporations with the GDP of economically small or modest-sized states. Such comparisons are wholly misleading. For one thing, the relevant measure of enterprise output, in this context, is not turnover but value added, which is the measure of a firm's contribution to world GDP. Value added is always below turnover, often substantially so. But the more fundamental objection is that such comparisons, now as in the past, have no bearing on the relative power disposed of by governments and businesses.

The idea that globalisation has greatly or even significantly reduced the power of governments to choose and act has little basis. Aside from such constraints on external economic policies as they have freely accepted and wish to maintain, national states today remain almost as free to act and take decisions as they were ten, twenty or thirty years ago.[4] Even small states, provided they

---

4 Arguments and evidence in support of this statement are well set out in the final chapter of Razeen Sally's illuminating book, *Classical Liberalism and International Economic Order*, Routledge, London, 1999, and in Martin Wolf, 'Will the Nation-State Survive Globalization?', *Foreign Affairs*, 80, 2001. Chapter 5 of *Misguided Virtue* also deals with these issues, and has been drawn on here.

have effective governments, retain the power to run their affairs in relation to such matters as defence, foreign policy, constitutional arrangements, the electoral system and voting rights, residence, citizenship, the legal system, public provision for health, pensions and welfare, the status of the national language or languages, and also, with the reservation just made, external economic policies. Even in relation to determining taxation rates, the evidence clearly shows that governments retain substantial freedom of action: countries with relatively high rates have not been forced by globalisation to reduce them drastically. For the ten core OECD countries which had the highest ratios of tax revenues to GDP in 1992, the corresponding ratios for 2002 were lower in three cases, much the same in another three, and higher in the remaining four.[5] Altogether, the notion that has been advanced by some political scientists, that today's more economically integrated world is one of 'post-sovereign governance', is pure fantasy.[6]

As to businesses, and especially the much-maligned MNEs, it is often argued, or just taken for granted, that one effect of both globalisation and privatisation, a disturbing one, has been to confer on them substantial new powers. There is no basis for this belief. It is true that in so far as governments act to extend the scope of markets, and to make them more open to competition, the area of operation of private businesses, and the opportunities that are open to them, are widened. This has indeed been

---

5   The ratios are to be found in Table 27 of the *OECD Economic Outlook* for June 2003.

6   Such an assertion is to be found, for example, in an article by J. A. Scholte and others in the *Journal of World Trade* (1999), where it is further stated, absurdly, that 'Recent intensified globalization has broken the Westphalian mould of politics'. It should be added that the authors of *Walking the Talk* explicitly reject (pp. 44–6) any such extreme view.

the result of recent privatisations, as also of the further freeing of international trade and investment flows. But the purpose of such market-opening measures is not to make companies more powerful, *nor is that their effect*. When after 1960 it became possible to export iron ore from Australia, major opportunities opened up for new large-scale business ventures in Western Australia; but the firms that grasped these opportunities did not thereby acquire, and have not exercised, coercive or exploitative powers: they (or, in some cases, their successors) are simply free to engage in useful activities. The economic power of business is not measured, nor even indicated, by the share of GDP that originates in the private sector.

Generally speaking, the effect of liberalisation is in fact to curb the power of corporations, not to enhance it. Such economic power as businesses can exercise arises chiefly from the absence or weakness of effective competition from rivals. It is therefore eroded, rather than increased, in so far as markets are made freer and more competitive; and indeed, privatisation has had the effect of bringing to an end the monopoly power of the former public enterprises which themselves were businesses. Wider opportunities and stronger competitive pressures go together. Actions that provide for both give private businesses collectively a more extended sphere of action; but they also make the profits of individual companies more dependent on effective performance against rivals, rather than on any exercise of market power.

At the risk of labouring the obvious, let me add that today, just as ten or twenty years ago,

- it is governments, not businesses, however large, which make laws, levy taxes, and impose binding regulations;

- it is governments, not businesses, however large, which employ, and give orders to, armed forces and police;
- it is governments, not businesses, however large, which have a monopoly of coercive powers.

One might suppose that businesses and business organisations themselves, in their own defence against the many hostile critics who accuse them of wielding overweening and unaccountable power, would have stressed these obvious points; but in all too many cases they have acquiesced in, or even endorsed, the mistaken belief that globalisation has conferred on them both large unmerited gains and substantial new powers, by virtue of which they now have to assume new social obligations. In this as in some other ways, they have tolerated, or even lent support to, arguments, criticisms and forms of social pressure which they could and should have held out against.

I believe that events in recent years have in fact demonstrated how weak and vulnerable even the largest business enterprises are today. In the face of determined attacks from anti-market critics and activists, leading businesses and business organisations, with few exceptions, have put up little resistance. They have even failed to defend themselves effectively against completely unwarranted charges. Many of them now appear as convinced appeasers of their critics and opponents – some with resignation, others with equanimity or even relish.[7] One might question whether this is responsible conduct.

---

7   Supporting evidence for these statements is to be found in Robert Halfon's incisive essay *Corporate Irresponsibility: Are Businesses Appeasing Anti-Business Activist-sts?*, Social Affairs Unit, London, 1998, as also in *Misguided Virtue*.

'Global governance' and 'civil society'

A presumption that globalisation has had profound and disturbing effects, together with the mistaken notion that national governments have lost the power to control events and decide policies, often goes nowadays with a proposed blueprint for 'global governance'. This blueprint provides for substantially greater involvement of international businesses and so-called 'public interest' non-governmental organisations (the NGOs) in shouldering what are seen as the now heavier burdens of governance in a globalised world. There is to be a tripartite 'global partnership', in which governments (together with international agencies, which are sometimes separately identified as a fourth partner) join forces with business and 'civil society'.

Within the business world, a leading representative of this way of thinking is the influential World Economic Forum. In the report that it issued after its annual meeting for 2002, the Forum, speaking for the many international businesses and CEOs that support its activities and attend its meetings, asserted that:

> Transparent multi-stakeholder networks will likely emerge as the most legitimate form of global problem solving in the 21st century. Governments must join with business, international organizations and the emerging transnational civil society to form coalitions around critical challenges on the global agenda and collaborate in flexible frameworks to resolve them.

Again, the reader is told on the dust jacket of *Walking the Talk* that: 'a global partnership – between governments, business and civil society – is essential, if accelerating moves towards globalization are to maximize opportunities for all – especially the world's poor'. Not surprisingly, such ideas are likewise endorsed by most

NGOs and UN agencies, as well as by many commentators and political figures.

In these writings, as in many others of their kind, including official statements from governments and international agencies, the term 'civil society' is given a restricted interpretation. It is taken to refer only to the NGOs – that is, to a range of organisations that includes consumer associations, conservation and environmental groups, societies concerned with economic development in poor countries, human rights groups, movements for social justice, humanitarian societies, organisations representing indigenous peoples, and church groups from all denominations. But to identify these various organisations with 'civil society' is a misuse of language, since the term should be given, and historically has been given, a much broader meaning. This now prevalent usage confers on these groups a representative status which is not rightly theirs.

The idea of a global partnership has been put into effect through the Global Compact, launched in 1999 by the Secretary-General of the United Nations. Within the Compact, participating businesses and business organisations commit themselves to acting in accordance with a set of nine principles: these derive from various international resolutions, and relate to the observance of human rights, the establishment and upholding of labour standards, and protection of the environment. Business participants are to work in conjunction with UN agencies, and with selected NGOs and trade unions, in defining, interpreting and giving expression to these principles: the aim is 'to craft cooperative solutions to the challenges of globalization' (*Walking the Talk*, p. 168). Several hundred businesses and business organisations have now become participants in the Compact, alongside trade unions and NGOs.

There are obvious grounds for questioning whether a new corporatist 'global partnership' has indeed become 'essential' to the economic progress of poor countries:

- First, in so far as the case for such an arrangement rests on the mistaken belief that power has passed from governments to businesses, it has no basis.
- Second, the economic history of the past half-century, summarised above, shows that many poor countries have been able to make rapid and sustained economic progress in the absence of any such institutional arrangement. How is it that the more successful developing and transition countries, where notable advances have been made and are continuing to be made entirely without benefit of any 'global partnership', have now become critically dependent on such an initiative for their future advancement?
- Third, it is far from clear, to put it no more strongly, just how a partnership of this kind could significantly improve the situation and prospects of the many faltering economies. When, as in most of these countries, the background conditions for sustained economic progress are at present unfulfilled, it would do little or nothing to aid in the formidable task of establishing them.

There is no reason whatever to believe that a new era has dawned, in which the economic prospects of poor countries have become largely dependent, as never before, on a conscious commitment by the MNEs, in alliance with other elements within 'the international community', to come to their assistance.

None of this is to deny or to minimise either the plight of many faltering economies or the extent of poverty in the world of today; nor is it to suggest that the governments and peoples of rich countries are already doing the most that could reasonably be expected of them to help, which is certainly not the case. But the proposals now made by the business and other advocates of 'global governance' are based on a total misreading of events and relationships.

The case against international corporatism

Viewed in the light of historical evidence, the notion of a new corporatist global partnership may appear simply as unfounded and irrelevant. But in fact it is worse than that. Attempts to translate the notion into practice are liable to do more harm than good, for three related reasons.

Reason number one is constitutional. The authors of *Walking the Talk*, in a chapter headed 'From dialogue to partnership', write approvingly (p. 162) of 'new approaches to governance', which would involve 'balancing the roles, responsibilities, accountabilities and capabilities of different levels of governments and different actors or sectors in society'. But the whole notion of an equal global partnership between governments and non-governmental organisations is inadmissible, and holds out dangers for the democratic process. No non-governmental organisation, and no grouping of such organisations, has a valid claim to represent, and to speak for, the people of a country when that country has a democratically elected and responsible government: persons who are not elected, and who are not accountable to a duly elected and broadly representative legislature, can have no such status. Neither NGOs nor businesses – nor trade unions for that matter – have valid claims *in their own right* to play an active role in international negotiations and decision-making. Of course, they have well-founded claims to have their arguments heard and considered by public authorities, and to be informed and consulted by them. But responsibility for the conduct of substantive discussions and negotiations, and for the determination of policies, should rest with those holding office in elected governments, and with the officials who are appointed to serve and act for them. Governments are free, if they consider it advisable, to bring in representatives of business organisations or trade unions or NGOs as advisers, or even as full participants, in these proceedings. But that is for them to decide.

Reason number two for questioning the idea of a tripartite or quadripartite global partnership relates to the characteristic views both of the NGOs and the international agencies chiefly concerned. The great majority, if not all, of those NGOs that aspire to a larger role in global governance are opposed to freedom of cross-border trade and capital flows, suspicious of further moves in that direction (except possibly for unilateral trade concessions by rich to poor countries), and preoccupied with what they see as the damaging effects of globalisation. These attitudes typically go with a generalised hostility to capitalism, multinational enterprises and the idea of a market economy.[8] The decisive past and current contribution of business enterprises to economic progress, and the fact that this contribution has been made possible by the

---

8   David Robertson has made the point, in an article in *The World Economy*, 3(9), 2000, p. 1,132, that 'A search of NGOs' websites that claim to be part of "civil society" does not reveal any that support liberal trade'. The anti-liberal role of the NGOs in relation to the ill-fated Multilateral Agreement on Investment (MAI) is reviewed in my 1999 essay *The MAI Affair: A Story and Its Lessons*, published in 1999 by the Royal Institute of International Affairs, London, and the New Zealand Business Roundtable.

maintenance and extension of competitive markets, are over-looked, denied or played down. Much the same view of the world is to be found in UN agencies.

Reason number three for querying the notion of 'global part-nership' is that action taken under this heading may lead to over-regulation of the world. Should such a trend take hold, the most serious effects would be felt in poor countries.

The over-regulation in question would take the form of laying down, and enforcing, common or uniform international norms, standards, rules and codes. The pressure for this may come from governments, as in the case of the European Union, where the European Commission has recently endorsed the dubious notion of 'global social governance'. It may also come from international agencies, with the acquiescence or support of their member governments. But similar results may follow from actions taken by MNEs on their own account. These businesses are now under strong social pressures, first, to adopt themselves, throughout their operations, high self-chosen environmental and 'social' standards, and second, to ensure that these same standards are met by their partners, suppliers and contractors – and even, on some interpretations, by their business customers.

Any such trend towards imposed uniformity, whether offi-cially or unofficially promoted, is liable to do harm. Since circum-stances vary greatly across countries, the whole notion of common cross-border standards, or even of universal minima, is open to question. In so far as pressures for greater uniformity become effective, they will restrict the potential for mutual gains through trade. In particular, such developments would worsen the pros-pects of people in developing countries, by depriving them of employment opportunities which they would be glad to take.

To adopt this way of 'giving capitalism a human face' will reduce welfare, especially though not only in the poorest countries where terms and conditions of employment that are fully acceptable to the workers concerned can be represented as being exploitative and immoral. Regulation, whether formal or informal, as also prudent reluctance by MNEs to involve themselves in deals or arrangements within poor countries that may make them subject to fierce, sustained and damaging attacks by anti-business activists, will tend to close off a range of what would be mutually beneficial market-based transactions. The authors of *Walking the Talk* assert (p. 42) that 'Denying poor people access to markets is planet-destroying as well as people-destroying'; but denial of opportunities for poor people is a predictable result of the forms of 'global governance' that they and the firms they speak for have endorsed.

The enforcement of, or tacit acquiescence in, norms and standards which are unrelated to local market conditions will in fact have the opposite effect to that claimed for it. As Martin Wolf has noted in his column in the *Financial Times* (2 December 1999), 'A dynamic international economy already has a human face. Its humanity resides in the opportunities that it offers to ordinary people.'

The primary role confirmed

To sum up: the idea that the globalisation of recent years has led to a decisive break with the past is mistaken. Closer international economic integration is not a new development but a long-established trend. Its further progress in the past ten to fifteen years, to which the label of 'globalisation' has been attached, did not mark the dawn of a new era. Globalisation has not created a borderless world, deprived national governments of their powers to act, made MNEs significantly and disturbingly more powerful, worsened the situation or prospects of faltering economies, or created a need for new mechanisms of global governance in which business and 'civil society' would work as equal partners with governments and UN agencies. Rather, it has taken farther already existing tendencies towards greater freedom of international cross-border trade and investment flows; and in so doing, it has brought gains to people in all those countries, rich and poor, where market economies are sufficiently developed for business enterprises to be able to profit from the change. In this process the primary role of business, as sketched out in the previous chapter, has neither been undermined nor put in question: to the contrary, it has been confirmed and reinforced. The further liberalisation of cross-border transactions, in recent years as in the past, has both opened up new opportunities for enterprises to innovate and strengthened the competitive pressures on them to do so. Globalisation in this sense does not at all give rise to the need for a new charter for businesses, a new 'licence to operate' to be conferred by 'society'. Rather, it both enables and constrains them to perform more effectively their already established primary role, as agents of change within a market economy.

This interpretation of events is not generally accepted. Although recent globalisation, accurately seen, provides neither justification nor support for the doctrine of CSR, the belief that it does so is widely held. The spread of this conviction can best be understood against a more extended background: the popularity of CSR today forms a distinctive new element within a broader trend of thinking which can be traced much farther back. The main pressures for the adoption of CSR by businesses have arisen, not from actual recent developments on the world economic scene, correctly perceived and interpreted, but from the way in which the general climate of opinion has evolved in relation to international economic and environmental issues. This evolution forms the subject matter of the next chapter.

4   GLOBAL SALVATIONISM AND CONSENSUS PRESSURES

Two strands of salvationist thinking

Over the past half-century, two strands of thinking about world problems have been much in evidence and have received continuing support. The first relates to problems of poverty and economic development, and the second to environmental issues. In both, two elements are combined. One is a generally dark – not to say alarmist – picture of the world's current state and future prospects, at any rate unless timely and far-reaching changes are made. The second element is a conviction that remedies for the present highly alarming situation are known, and that they require the adoption by governments and 'the international community' of concerted strategies and programmes. 'Solutions' are at hand, given wise collective decisions and actions. It is the combination of alarmist visions with confidently radical collectivist prescriptions for the world as a whole which characterises *global salvationism*.

Gradually, the two strands have drawn closer, so that they have now effectively merged to form a salvationist consensus; and over the past ten to fifteen years the consensus has gained in influence, because it has acquired new aspects and sources of strength. This recent evolution of ideas, perceptions and institutions has brought with it, among other things, the emergence of, and growing support for, the doctrine of CSR.

Rich and poor on Planet Earth

As to the first strand, one aspect of 'development pessimism', long established but still flourishing, is a misleading treatment of cross-country differences in real income per head and the factors that give rise to them. A conspicuous recent instance is to be found in *Walking the Talk*. The authors assert (p. 41) that 'Some 80% of people live in developing countries and *have to live* off 20% of *the planet's goods*' (italics mine). Here there are three basic errors. First, the 80–20 comparison is made (though not explicitly) in terms of GDP measured at market exchange rates. It therefore takes no account of differences in price levels as between countries, which have to be allowed for if genuine comparisons of GDP and GDP per head are to be made. If for example one takes Maddison's GDP estimates, in which these inter-country differences are corrected by the use of purchasing power parity exchange rates, the share of world GDP in 2000 accounted for by the 80 per cent of people living in poorer countries appears, not as 20 per cent, but as approximately 37 per cent. Second, the impression is conveyed that the goods and services that people, businesses and governments currently buy are somehow made available by 'the planet' and then unequally – and hence inequitably – distributed among countries. In fact, rich countries are rich because their citizens produce more per head, not because they have secured privileged access to 'the planet's goods', or to its 'resources'. Third, the argument implies that in the world of today developing countries are fated to stay poor unless they are rescued from this condition by being allocated more of the planet's bounty, whereas history demonstrates that this is not the case.

These are elementary points, but they have eluded not only business leaders in the WBCSD and elsewhere, but also other influential persons and organisations. For example, the president of the World Bank, James Wolfensohn, decried not long ago the state of mind that 'allowed us to view as normal a world where fewer than 15 per cent of us – in rich countries – dominate the world's wealth and take [sic] 80 per cent of its dollar income'.[1] In his 2002 presidential address to the American Association for the Advancement of Science, Professor Peter H. Raven, distancing himself still further from the facts, spoke of 'a world in which 20% of us control [sic] 80% of the resources [sic], and 80% of us have to make do with the rest'.[2] Similarly misleading comparisons, based on GDP conversions using market exchange rates, are to be found in the last reports of both Working Group II and Working Group III of the Intergovernmental Panel on Climate Change (IPCC), as also in the recent *Global Environment Outlook 3*, published by the United Nations Environment Programme (UNEP), which is one of the two parent agencies of the IPCC.[3] Both these latter officially approved sources give a distorted picture of the international distribution of income, based on the use of market exchange rates for cross-country comparisons of GDP and GDP per head, despite the fact that the use of purchasing power parity rates for such comparisons was recommended in the 1993 System of National

1   Quoted from his foreword to the World Bank publication *World Development Indicators 2002*.

2   Peter H. Raven, 'Science, Sustainability, and the Human Prospect', *Science*, 9 June 2002.

3   *Climate Change 2001: Impacts, Adaptation and Vulnerability*, contribution of Working Group II to the Third Assessment Report of the Intergovernmental Panel on Climate Change, published for the IPCC in 2001 by Cambridge University Press, p. 477; *Climate Change 2001: Mitigation*, contribution of Working Group III to the Third Assessment Report, p. 87; and United Nations Environment Programme, *Global Environment Outlook 3: Past, present and future perspectives*, Earthscan, London, 2002, pp. 35–6.

Accounts (SNA), which was unanimously adopted by the UN Statistical Commission with the approval of the national statistical offices of member governments.[4] The UNEP and the IPCC, in the passages cited, have either disregarded this recommendation or failed to notice it.

Exaggerated representations of the gap between rich and poor countries, together with the false belief that the inequalities are due to a maldistribution of 'resources' (or 'the planet's goods') which are independently provided to mankind, lead naturally to two further premises, both mistaken. The first of these, already noted above in Chapter 2, is that the international differences result from, and are manifestations of, injustice. A second is that the situation of the poorest countries can be remedied only through collective measures and programmes which are already clearly identified and practicable, which require stronger and more equitably constituted forms of global governance, and for which the necessary resources have to be provided by the rich ('privileged') countries. Poor countries are viewed as largely dependent on outside help: their progress can be assured only through deliverance from above. Such arguments have long been the stock-in-trade of most of the UN agencies that are concerned with economic and development issues, and they have now been taken over by many NGOs and representatives of the business world. They fit well with the groundless belief, referred to in the previous chapter, that globalisation has marginalised poor countries.

In this way of thinking, the remarkable economic progress made by initially poor countries over the past half-century, and

---

4   The SNA was the combined product of five international organisations – the UN, the IMF, the World Bank, the OECD, and the European Commission.

the fact that generally speaking it has owed little or nothing to flows or programmes of assistance from outside, is ignored or mentioned only in passing: it does not fit the model. Again, the background conditions on which progress depends, as summarised in Chapter 2, are sidelined. While the evidence and lessons of history may not be explicitly denied, and are sometimes even acknowledged, the focus of attention is on new but well-specified collective 'solutions' for problems that are portrayed as otherwise intractable.

A similar way of thinking has long entered into the case argued by the governments of developing countries in international meetings and negotiations. These governments, along with the various UN agencies concerned, have consistently stressed the need for unreciprocated assistance and concessions by the OECD countries, in the form of aid flows, debt relief, unilateral market opening, preferential trade agreements, special arrangements for the transfer of technologies, support for commodity prices, and exemption of the developing countries from the rules and disciplines which the OECD member states have accepted within the framework of what is now the WTO. Here again, the historical record, of widespread and in many cases outstanding economic progress in poor countries that has neither depended on nor resulted from such unilateral assistance and concessions, is largely ignored. Although this official bias is partly explained by the negotiating context, and the understandable desire within it to bring pressure to bear on OECD member governments to make concessions, it also reflects a genuinely held view of what economic development requires. In this view, both the gains from freer trade and investment flows and the extent to which development depends on internal factors are played down or left unmentioned.[5]

Environmental concerns and the salvationist consensus

The second strand relates to environmental issues. Ever since World War II, there have been frequent expressions of concern that human behaviour, and in particular the evolution of economic systems, would before long give rise to serious or even disastrous consequences. Such fears have been voiced regularly by eminent scientists. These and other commentators have viewed with alarm the growth of world population and output, and predicted both the running down or exhaustion of natural resources and the inability of world food production to keep pace with population because of pressures on available land. Warnings of disaster have been commonplace.

Alongside these earlier voices, which were chiefly academic although some alarmist publications sold well, there developed from the 1960s onward a broader and more popular line of thinking and action, in the form of the environmental movement. As John McCormick has put it, 'The concerns of a few scientists, administrators and conservation groups blossomed into a fervent mass movement that swept the industrialized world.'[6] Since then the movement has gained ground, not just with public opinion

---

5   Of course, this way of thinking has not been confined to governments of devel-
     oping countries. It forms the main theme of Deepak Lal's notable critique, *The
     Poverty of Development Economics*, Institute of Economic Affairs, London, 3rd edn,
     2001.

6   John McCormick, *The Global Environmental Movement: Reclaiming Paradise*, Bel-
     haven Press, London, 1989, p. 47.

but also within governments and international agencies, while its more moderate members and their increasingly influential NGOs have joined forces with environmentally concerned scientists.

Over the past 25 to 30 years there has been a coming together of the two strands of thinking, developmental and environmental. That they represented two aspects of the same set of urgent world problems, and should be treated as such both intellectually and administratively, was a constant theme of influential authors such as the late Barbara Ward, as also of international gatherings and the agencies and government departments sponsoring them, from the late 1960s onward: the decision to establish the UNEP, taken at the 1972 Stockholm Conference on the Human Environment – the first of its kind – marks the first clear manifestation of this tendency.[7] The thinking that enters into the fusion of the two can be illustrated by a quotation from a mid-1970s study, whose wording can still be taken as representative of global salvationism today:

> Two gaps, steadily widening, appear to be at the heart
> of mankind's present crises: the gap between man and
> nature, and the gap between 'North' and 'South', rich and
> poor. Both gaps must be narrowed if world-shattering
> catastrophes are to be avoided; but they can be narrowed
> only if global 'unity' and Earth's 'finiteness' are explicitly
> recognized.[8]

---

7   Barbara Ward was the principal author, in conjunction with the French scientist René Dubos, of an unofficial report commissioned by the Secretary-General of the Stockholm Conference, which served as the main single working document for it. The report was published in 1972 (Penguin, London) under the title *Only One Earth: The Care and Maintenance of a Small Planet*.

8   Mihajlo Mesarovic and Eduard Pestel, *Mankind at the Turning Point: The Second Report to the Club of Rome*, Hutchinson, London, 1975, p. ix.

Leading businesses and business organisations have lent uncritical support to global salvationist assumptions and beliefs. This tendency is exemplified in *Walking the Talk*, not only in what is said about globalisation and the situation of poor countries, already referred to above, but also in the authors' treatment of environmental issues. These are specifically covered in two chapters, one on 'eco-efficiency' and the other entitled 'Reflecting the worth of the earth'. The text presents a sombre view of current environmental trends and prospects: this is reflected, for example, in the statement (p. 242) that 'we are steadily eroding the planet's ability to support us' and the reference (p. 84) to 'the tide of damage to the natural environment as populations grow and the poor nations develop'. As with the treatment of globalisation and poverty, the emphasis of the book is on 'planetary anxieties' which it does not seriously question. This alarmist bias is in line with other documents and reports that have emerged in recent years from in and around the business world. In such writings, little account is taken of the work of those authors, such as the late Julian Simon and, more recently, Bjørn Lomborg, who have argued that past and present widely accepted visions of environmental deterioration and disaster do not accord with the evidence.[9] (The disturbingly intemperate attacks that have been made on the work of both Simon and Lomborg have chiefly come, however, not from the business world, but from academic scientists and from NGOs and their members.[10])

---

9   In Simon's work, the main single reference is to *The Ultimate Resource 2*, published in 1996 by the Princeton University Press. Lomborg's *The Skeptical Environmentalist* was published in 2001 by Cambridge University Press.

10   The final chapter of *The Ultimate Resource 2* is an 'Epilogue' entitled 'My Critics and I'. In it Simon gives some depressing instances of what he terms 'the human propensity to suppress opposing views'. The same propensity, and the same

In endorsing both developmental and environmental pessimism, the business advocates of CSR form part of a wider movement of opinion. They have joined forces with NGOs, academics, commentators who are concerned with environmental or development issues, officials in government departments that are responsible for handling those issues, and virtually all international agencies including the European Commission. All these are parties to today's salvationist consensus.

Salvationism reinforced

One might reasonably suppose that the course of events in recent years, or even over the whole of the past half-century, would have weakened the hold of global salvationist ideas. The various crises and disasters so often and freely predicted have not come to pass. Across the world, prosperity has grown and spread in ways that have no parallel in history; and partly in consequence, there have been widespread and substantial improvements in the quality of life and the environment (though improvements are not the whole story). Hundreds of millions of people in poor countries have made significant or even dramatic advances, without benefit of global strategies, partnerships and programmes offering 'empowerment' and deliverance from above, largely because individuals and enterprises in those countries were able to create and exploit economic opportunities. In the many poor countries where little or no progress has been made, the main reasons can be seen to

intolerance, have been evinced in relation to Lomborg's book. It should be added, however, that not all the dissenting critics of the two authors have written in this vein.

lie in deep-seated internal problems, or corrupt and repressive regimes, which have prevented the establishment of adequately functioning market economies. The collapse of communism has discredited centralised economic planning, and provided further evidence that it is only within the framework of a market economy that economic progress can be relied on. These events have belied the salvationist vision.

Up to a point, all this evidence has had its effect on people and governments – for example, in making some of them rather more aware of, and receptive to, arguments for liberalising economies. But on balance, over the past ten to fifteen years, salvationist ways of thinking have become more influential rather than less. They form a prominent part of the background against which the obligations of businesses, legal and moral, are now considered and defined. Five mutually reinforcing developments have contributed to this evolution of opinion.

The first of these, already commented on in the previous chapter, is the remarkable growth and spread of ill-founded notions concerning the effects of recent globalisation.

Second is the rise in status and influence of the NGOs. This rise is not only, nor even mainly, a matter of individual membership and support, though these have indeed grown. Almost everywhere, NGOs have increasingly been brought by governments and international agencies into more or less formal consultative and collaborative processes. Some have been assigned roles as executing agencies for official aid projects. As advisers and executors, NGOs that are officially recognised receive public funding. The Internet has provided all of them with a means of highlighting issues and mounting public campaigns, as in the well-orchestrated attacks that were made on the Multilateral Agreement on Investment (MAI).[11] They now have an assured place in most international meetings, and there are proposals for expanding further their status and role in the work of international agencies.

Businesses generally, and large multinational enterprises in particular, now go out of their way to inform, consult and where possible cooperate with NGOs that they view as relatively moderate. Increasingly, they are inclined to think of these organisations not just as critics who must be answered but as partners in a common endeavour. Thus the authors of *Walking the Talk* note approvingly that NGOs, as a form of 'external accountability', 'can be harnessed as a powerful driver for internal change' (p. 140). Among the many citations in *Misguided Virtue*, perhaps the most surprising, and disturbing, is taken from an article published in 2000 by Sir Mark Moody-Stuart, then CEO of Shell. On behalf of Shell, Moody-Stuart wrote: '... because we too are concerned at the requirement to address those in poverty who are excluded [*sic*] from the benefits that many of us share in the global economy, *we share the objective of the recent demonstrators in Seattle, Davos and Prague*' (italics added). Soon afterwards, Sir Mark retired from his position at Shell. Since then he has been appointed chairman of Anglo-American, the large international mining company, and was chosen by the international business community to lead the business delegation to the 2002 Johannesburg World Summit on Sustainable Development.

11　It is the not the case, however, that the campaign waged by the NGOs against the MAI was responsible for the failure to conclude the Agreement. OECD governments brought the negotiations to an end for their own reasons. The far-reaching liberalisation of foreign direct investment flows originally envisaged proved to be several bridges too far.

A third influential factor has been the spread and intensification of various forms of egalitarian concern. Modern salvationists characteristically pay little regard to the past record of economic progress and its lessons, but focus instead on the perceived inequalities of today which they see as evidence of remediable injustice. They portray the modern world as thickly populated with the deprived, marginalised and excluded. These latter are people whose plight is seen as unaffected, or even on some interpretations largely created, by the operation of 'unfettered' markets. They include poor people everywhere, including the relatively poor in rich countries, and employees in general, who as ever are seen as being at the mercy of grasping profit-motivated businesses. This is not all, however. More recent additions to the list of victims are women, ethnic minorities, gays and lesbians, children, the aged, those who are handicapped or have disabilities, local communities and indigenous peoples.

The increasing influence of radical egalitarianism largely helps to explain the substantial erosion of freedom of contract which has occurred in many countries in recent decades. On the international scene, egalitarian doctrines have been endorsed by most international agencies, with strong backing from NGOs and either support or acquiescence not only from member governments of the agencies but also, and increasingly, from businesses and business organisations. These various elements are now broadly united in accepting and propagating a picture of reality in which two notions are dominant. The first is that human economic activities, chiefly motivated by greed and profit, now present a dire threat to the planet. The second is that people everywhere, with the exception of prosperous white heterosexual males of working age and with no disabilities, are actual or potential victims whose welfare chiefly depends on laws, regulations and programmes introduced and enforced on their behalf by 'society' or 'the international community'.[12] In both its assumptions and its implications, this way of thinking is deeply collectivist, and it disregards completely the evidence and lessons of economic history. Within the business milieu, it is reflected in the belief of many CSR advocates that it has now become the duty of companies to take a leading role in rescuing excluded persons everywhere, in a world where such persons, in vast and arguably growing numbers, are dependent on outside help which governments are no longer fully competent to provide. In today's world of CSR, such delusions have acquired the status of orthodoxy.

A fourth influence, which began to make itself felt from the mid-1980s onward, has been concern about climate change and its possible consequences. This led to the establishment by governments in 1988 of the IPCC: it has the status of an intergovernmental body, as a joint subsidiary of UNEP and the World Meteorological Organisation. Since the IPCC's creation, concerns about the likelihood and impact of global warming have been reinforced by the analysis and projections contained in the three successive multi-volume Assessment Reports which it has so far published. What is more, these concerns have been accepted as soundly based by governments across the world. At the 1992 UN Conference on Environment and Development (the Rio 'Earth Summit'), 153 governments agreed on the UN Framework Convention on Climate Change; and the text of this Convention 'accepts that climate change is a serious problem, requiring a

---

12 Once the fit and prosperous white males grow old enough, they too become potential victims, whose rights have to be upheld by laws and regulations against discrimination on grounds of age.

"precautionary approach"... '[13] Within the Framework, action has been taken through the Kyoto Protocol of 1997, which incorporates specific commitments by industrial countries to curb emissions of greenhouse gases. Thus the possibility of unintended and damaging climate change, arising from human actions, is widely seen both as a valid reason for 'planetary anxiety' and as an argument for new mechanisms of global governance.

Issues relating to the causes, likelihood and possible consequences of global climate change fall outside the scope of this book. It is worth noting, however, that in its treatment of economic issues the IPCC process has incorporated leading elements of salvationist thinking. As seen above, some of its authors, and one of its two parent agencies, have quoted as valid distorted measures of the differences in GDP per head between rich and poor countries. Working groups associated with the IPCC have also endorsed the view that these international inequalities are to be viewed as manifestations of remediable injustice. Both presumptions have influenced projections that have been made for the Third Assessment Review of future world economic growth and greenhouse gas emissions.[14]

---

13 The quotation is from Michael Grubb et al., *The Earth Summit Agreements: A Guide and Assessment*, Earthscan, London, 1993.

14 For these and other reasons, Ian Castles and I have argued that the economic aspects of the IPCC's work need to be placed on a professionally sounder basis. The case is made in our article 'Economics, Emissions Scenarios and the Work of the IPCC', *Energy and Environment*, 14(4), 2003. In part, this article is a response to criticisms of our position that had been made, by fifteen authors involved in the work on emissions scenarios for the IPCC, in the previous issue of the same journal. More recently, a partly overlapping group of eighteen authors has contributed to that journal a further article by way of 'final response' on their part. In December 2003 the IPCC itself issued to the world a special press release dismissing our arguments. In this revealing document Castles and I are described as 'so-called "two independent commentators"', and as originators of 'some disinformation [that] has been spread questioning the scenarios'.

The fifth main factor reinforcing the hold of global salvationism has been the increasing and now general acceptance across the world, as a guiding principle for all, of the notion of sustainable development. From the 1970s onward, this notion began to enter into the vocabulary of the environmental strand of salvationist thinking, since it seemed fitting to label as unsustainable a process which (as it was argued) involved depletion of non-renewable resources, destruction of species and habitats, and the creation of increasingly unmanageable problems of pollution and waste. In the late 1980s the term came into more general use, and acceptance, after it had been made the centrepiece of the 1987 report of the UN World Commission on Environment and Development (the Brundtland Report). By this time it had been enlarged in scope, so as to include developmental as well as environmental goals: sustainable development was now taken to involve a closing of the gap between rich and poor. It became the watchword, the focus, of the salvationist consensus; and as such, it was the main theme and the central organising principle of the 1992 Rio 'Earth Summit'.

The Rio meeting brought a notable gain, not only for the concept of sustainable development but also for consensus ways of thinking. For the first time, an international conference on this range of topics was attended and supported by heads of state and heads of government: over 120 of these actually came to Rio. The various agreed resolutions and decisions thus acquired an extra authority which earlier documents of a similar kind had lacked. In large part, this resulted from the new and widely shared official concerns about the possibilities and risks of future climate change; but these concerns were incorporated, as an additional reinforcing element, into the already existing dark salvationist message which up till then had not been so generally endorsed. In the Rio documents and resolutions, this routine standard message was neither qualified nor watered down. It was given clear and undiluted expression in the agreed programme of action that was adopted at the summit, entitled *Agenda 21*. The preamble to this document opens as follows: 'Humanity stands at a defining moment in history. We are confronted with a perpetuation of disparities within and between nations, a worsening of poverty, hunger, ill health and illiteracy, and the continued deterioration of the ecosystems on which we depend for our well-being.' The proposed remedies for the ills thus outlined were to be given effect through 'a new global partnership for sustainable development'. Such was the salvationist diagnosis and prescription which all the participating governments proved ready to accept, many of them at the highest level.

Since the Rio Summit, the ground thus won by salvationism, against the weight of economic evidence but without serious opposition, has been consolidated and extended. In particular, sustainable development has become the watchword of governments all over the world. International conferences pay tribute to it in their documentation and communiqués. In the United Kingdom, it was formally endorsed in a statement of policy by the then Conservative government in 1994, and under the present Labour government it has been further emphasised as the basis for government policies in general.[15] In France, there is now a minister for it. The notion is rarely questioned today, and then

---

15   The references here are: first, *Sustainable Development: The UK Strategy*, Her Majesty's Stationery Office, London, 1994; and second, *A Better Quality of Life: A Strategy for Sustainable Development in the United Kingdom*, Department of the Environment and Transport, London, 1997.

only by unrepresentative persons in universities and think tanks. It has conquered the world.

Four related features of this triumph of sustainable development are to be noted. First, its many proponents, official and unofficial, typically speak and write as though people everywhere were agreed on just what the concept means and how it is to be pursued and achieved. In fact, however, it is neither well defined nor above question.[16]

Second, its adoption as a guiding principle has gone together with uncritical acceptance of the dubious accompanying notion that it has three distinct aspects or dimensions – economic, environmental and social. In Britain the present government, in announcing its allegiance to sustainable development, specifically made the point that the notion was now to be interpreted as covering not only environmental and economic aspects, which had been the focus of the previous official statement of 1994, but 'social' aspects as well. Again, the OECD ministerial communiqué of 1999 included the statement that: 'The pursuit of sustainable development ... is a key objective for OECD countries. Achieving this objective requires the integration of economic, environmental and social considerations into policy-making ...' In fact, however, these are not watertight categories. *Most of the aspects that are labelled 'environmental' or 'social' are economic issues, for which economic analysis and criteria offer a means to integration.*

Third, the notion of sustainable development, thus interpreted, has moved from being the property of the consensus to become the watchword of virtually all. In particular, it has been endorsed by governments as a whole, as in the OECD commu-

---

16 This theme is taken somewhat farther in Chapter 3 of *Misguided Virtue*.

niqué just quoted, so that *every department of state is now committed to it*. This marks a significant gain for global salvationism: its central concept has been taken up by the world in general. In the process, the salvationist beliefs themselves have become more widely accepted, or, at least, now pass relatively unchallenged.

Fourth, the rise of sustainable development has led directly to that of CSR. As seen in Chapter 1, CSR is defined with reference to the pursuit by companies of sustainable development. The subtitle of *Walking the Talk* is 'the business case for sustainable development', and this wording echoes earlier WBCSD publications and many other treatments of the subject. Again, the notion of 'meeting the triple bottom line' derives from the distinction between what are misleadingly taken to be sustainable development's three separate aspects. Both in the business world and outside it, CSR is viewed as a means to an agreed end. It is defined, presented and advocated as a way of giving effect to sustainable development.

Social pressures: the primary role disregarded

The current pressures on businesses to adopt CSR can be seen as coming from three sources. First are anti-business activists and NGOs, ranging from those who are unrelentingly hostile to capitalism to those who would find it acceptable only in a radically new guise. They stand ready, as ever, to condemn business enterprises for what they depict as anti-social profit-oriented behaviour, and in a number of cases their campaigns have made an impact. They cannot be ignored. Second are the more moderate elements within the consensus. These are more favourable to business and capitalism; and many of them are to be found within the business world, where CSR is often seen as a positive opportunity rather than, or as well as, a prudent response to critics. In varying degrees, these persons share the global salvationist view of the state of the world; and they wish to see companies take on a wider role, and adopt broader environmental and 'social' objectives, as part of an attempt by the international community to improve the outlook for humanity and the planet. Last are those who, though not subscribers to the consensus, have accepted or acquiesced in the enthronement of sustainable development and are aware that CSR can be linked to it. This latter category would seem to include ministries of finance and economics across the world, in so far as they have noticed what has been happening around them. On the other side, there has so far been little by way of open opposition to CSR, whether from within the business world or outside it.

As part of this recent evolution of opinion, governments individually and collectively have underwritten CSR. It has been formally commended by the European Commission, with the approval of the EU Council of Ministers.[17] In the recently revised version of the OECD's *Guidelines for Multinational Enterprises*, the new text is presented as 'a tool for promoting corporate social responsibility'. In the agreed 'outcome' document of the 2002 UN conference in Monterrey on 'financing for development', the participating governments said: 'We urge businesses to take into account not only the economic and financial but also the developmental, social, gender and environmental implications of their undertakings' (para. 23). In the UK, there is a minister charged with the responsibility for promoting CSR; and in May 2004

---

17 See the Commission's Green Paper, published in 2001, entitled *Promoting a European Framework for Corporate Social Responsibility*.

the government announced that, as from the next financial year, all British quoted companies would be 'required to issue a new annual corporate social responsibility statement' (*Financial Times*, 5 May 2004). Within international agencies, CSR has gained recognition and support not only at United Nations headquarters and in specialised UN agencies, but also in the World Bank Group and the OECD.

In the face of these various forms of pressure – internal and external, official and unofficial, hostile, neutral and friendly – it is not surprising that many businesses, and MNEs in particular, have made a positive response. For many of these firms it would be difficult, and arguably unwise, for them to hold out against the pressures even if they were inclined to do so, which in many cases they are not. They are concerned, not only to safeguard their reputations in the face of damaging charges by outside critics, but also to take account of the views, wishes and expectations of a wider set of people and institutions, including many in the business world itself. In endorsing CSR, business enterprises, business organisations and business commentators have reflected, and responded to, a climate of opinion in which a particular conception of sustainable development, largely arising out of the ideas of global salvationism, has become widely accepted as a guiding principle and slogan. One might argue that many of the companies involved had, and still have, little alternative but to act in this way.

As against such a conclusion, some of the critics of CSR – they are not a numerous breed – would agree with the view expressed by Milton Friedman over forty years ago:

> Few trends could so thoroughly undermine the very
> foundations of our free society as the acceptance by
> corporate officials of a social responsibility other than to

> make as much money for their stockholders as possible.
> This is a fundamentally subversive doctrine. If businessmen
> do have a social responsibility other than making maximum
> profits for stockholders, how are they to know what it is?
> Can self-selected private individuals know what the social
> interest is?[18]

But although Friedman's questions are good ones, today's adherents of CSR can provide answers to them. They can say, correctly so far as it goes, that it is not just 'self-selected' business persons but also strong elements of public opinion, together with the governments of at any rate the OECD countries, which view sustainable development as giving expression to the 'social interest' and CSR as a means to realising it. (More on this, however, in the next chapter.) They can further maintain that it is actually in the interests of stockholders (shareholders) if businesses take this course. The argument here is – as stated in Chapter 1 – that profits depend largely on reputation, and reputation today depends on being seen to be doing the right thing by promoting sustainable development. If so, then over the longer term at any rate it is precisely by adopting CSR that modern businesses will 'make as much money for their stockholders as possible'.

However, accounting for the rise of CSR, recognising the various social pressures behind it, and noting that counter-arguments can be brought against a fundamental objection to it, is not the same as justifying its general adoption. For two related reasons, the story does not end at this point.

First, in ways that have been set out above, the view of the world and of past history which enters into global salvationism,

---

18 *Capitalism and Freedom*, University of Chicago Press, 1962, p. 133.

and which underlies many of the arguments for CSR, is biased and distorted. It presents a dark and alarmist picture in which international inequalities are greatly exaggerated, poor countries are portrayed as victims whose progress chiefly depends on deliverance from above, the impact of globalisation is both overstated and misrepresented, questionable corporatist schemes for 'global governance' are uncritically endorsed, and environmental issues are treated predominantly with reference to problems, threats and potential disasters. It glosses over the impressive record of gains in material welfare during this past half-century, in poor countries as well as rich, the fact that the pace and extent of this progress have been strongly influenced by the actions and policies of national governments, the part played by market-based arrangements and institutions in making progress possible, and the contribution that has been made by the freeing of international trade and capital flows. It is one-sided, uninformed and unhistorical.

Second, and as part of this misleading picture of economic events and relationships, *the salvationist perspective largely ignores the long-established primary role of business.* The business contribution to economic progress is played down, in part because the extent of that progress is itself not fully acknowledged. The fact that this contribution is made possible by the combination of opportunities and pressures which only a competitive market economy can provide is likewise given too little weight, or else simply disregarded.

There are in fact two distinct kinds of pressures that are now brought to bear on businesses. First, and as always, there are the market-originating or *competitive* pressures, which are impersonal. As noted in Chapter 2, these act as drivers to better enterprise performance, all the more so because they go together with the business opportunities which economic freedom opens up. The effective execution of the primary role of business depends on them. Alongside these competitive pressures are the *social* pressures which are brought to bear by public opinion, and which are now exemplified by the pressure on businesses to take the path of CSR. Apart from some violent extremes, these latter pressures are legitimate, in the sense of being within the law; and they have to be taken into account even when they have not found expression in legislation and official regulations. It is not to be assumed, however, that accommodating them will strengthen the primary role of business: *such is not their purpose, and it may well not be their effect.* As will be seen below, the general adoption of CSR could serve to neutralise or weaken market pressures and thus undermine the primary role.

In any case, the fact that today's social pressures on businesses to take the path of CSR come from many sources, and are generally within the law, does not mean that they are well founded. That they are so closely linked to a distorted view of economic history and economic relationships is reason for doubt. In so far as the public and official opinion favouring CSR is wedded to global salvationist beliefs and assumptions that have little or no basis, it should be questioned, rather than taken for granted and acceded to.

In order to explore these issues further, it is helpful to look more closely at the situation of individual businesses, and to consider in that context three related questions. One is the uses and limitations, from the standpoint of the public interest, of enterprise profitability as a goal or criterion. A second is the claims now made for sustainable development, as an alternative basis for viewing and assessing the contribution of business enterprises to the general welfare, and hence for guiding business conduct and redefining corporate responsibilities. Third is the motivation and values of business leaders and the firms that they direct. In this latter context, I consider the question of how closely the business contribution to the general welfare is linked to individual motives other than self-interest and to enterprise concerns that go beyond profitability. These various themes are taken up in the chapter that follows.

5   PROFITS, WELFARE AND VIRTUE

I begin by returning to the work and role of Lang Hancock. His main achievement lay in the leading part he played in making possible the spectacular development of iron ore mining in the Pilbara. An American business associate wrote of him, at the time when this achievement was taking shape, that 'From the start he had the vision, the comprehension and the faith that was required to set the stage for the development of these resources on a scale commensurate with their value'. But while recognising Hancock's contribution, and the insight and determination that underlay it, one may pose a question concerning the Pilbara developments, a question that can equally be asked of other business ventures. How can we tell whether, and to what extent, they have made a positive contribution to the general welfare?

Profits and the general welfare: an economic approach

This is a simple and challenging question which has no simple answer. But within a competitive market economy there is a helpful first-approximation answer, both in the Pilbara case and in others like it. In such an economy, the primary test, or criterion, is that of *profitability*. The benefits to people in general that arise from a business venture are indicated by what they show themselves prepared to pay for the outputs that result from it

– that is, by the revenues that accrue to the business. On the other side of the account, the cost to people in general of the venture is the value to them of what could have been produced if the resources absorbed by the venture had been deployed elsewhere; and although this figure cannot be known, a reasonable first approximation to it is the costs actually incurred by the business. Profits are the difference between these two flows, the benefits and the costs. Hence *they are a prima facie indicator – not a precise measure, but an indicator – of the good that a business is doing for people in general.* Viewed in this light, *they serve an essential signalling function in a market economy.*[1] If the Pilbara ventures had brought with them substantial losses for the businesses concerned, this would have given reason to question their whole validity, from a wider standpoint than that of the firms themselves. Of the many anti-market slogans that are now in vogue, the most misleading, and potentially the most damaging in its effects, is that of 'people before profits'. In a competitive market economy, profits can only be made through serving the wishes and interests of people. Within such an economy, enterprise profitability depends on performance in that service: *profits are performance-related.*

Of course, there are good reasons why this is far from being the last word on the subject, and why the test of profitability may be open to question in ways that an economic approach, of the kind just outlined, must allow for. Sir Samuel Brittan published some

---

1 More strictly, perhaps, the argument concerning welfare should be stated in terms of the sum total of consumer and producer surpluses arising from an economic activity or venture, rather than profits as such which can therefore at best be no more than an indicator. But as to the signalling function, there is no alternative to profits.

time ago a perceptive essay called *Two Cheers for Self-Interest*.[2] It is perhaps tempting to take over the phrase, by calling for 'two cheers for profits'. But this would be too simple a formula. The extent to which profits deserve applause can vary widely according to circumstances.

In some circumstances, two cheers would be over-generous. Profitability can be questionable or misleading as an indicator of social benefit, and the profit motive may lead businesses down paths which are dubious from a wider perspective even when the actions in question are both legal and undertaken in good faith. Two sources of 'contamination' of profits are well recognised in standard economic analysis.[3] One of these arises from the limitations of even a well-functioning competitive market economy, while the other relates to ways in which markets may be prevented from functioning as well as they might.

Under the first heading, the main problem is that of external effects, or '*externalities*'. These may arise from business operations, but they take effect outside them. They may be beneficial (positive) or harmful (negative). They impinge on aggregate material welfare in ways that are not fully reflected in the revenues or costs of the enterprises concerned: the prices paid for inputs, or received for outputs, fail to measure costs and gains at the margin to people in general. A widely cited example today of a negative externality

---

2   Samuel Brittan, *Two Cheers for Self-Interest*, Institute of Economic Affairs, London, 1985. Later issued, in revised form, as Chapter 2 of his book *Capitalism with a Human Face*, Edward Elgar, Cheltenham, 1995.

3   Not all economists would subscribe to this standard analysis, and the 'economic approach' of which it forms part. What I have termed 'an' (not 'the') economic approach is based on a way of thinking which comes more readily to economists than to others, but which some economists would question and some non-economists might cheerfully accept.

is the possibility – some would argue, the virtual certainty – that a set of prices which emerges from profit-directed actions and decisions by enterprises, in the absence of deliberate corrective adjustments, must fail to take account of probable effects on the global climate of greenhouse gas emissions arising from economic activity. In this case as in others, the corrective adjustments are designed to affect profitability calculations: in so doing, they lead firms to 'internalise externalities'. Within the economic approach described here, they are seen as being decided on, and imposed by, public authorities, rather than adopted voluntarily by businesses themselves.

Even if external effects are insignificant or properly taken into account, the profitability criterion may be open to question, because of restrictions that have been placed on competition and economic freedom and which limit both market opportunities and competitive pressures. Often, though by no means always, these restrictions arise from pressures on the part of interest groups including businesses themselves. Like other economic agents, companies individually and collectively may find it in their interest to improve their situation by restricting competition and free entry. They may try to achieve this on their own account, through restrictive agreements if these are legal or the laws against them are ineffective. But a more promising route to earning profits that are not performance-related is to obtain, and hold on to, special favours or dispensations from governments. These may take the form of tariffs, import levies and quotas, restrictive licensing, preferential access, curbs on foreign direct investment, subsidies, tax privileges and concessions, and divers forms of assistance in kind: the list is a long one. With some exceptions, such as those that are well designed to take account of genuine external effects, such measures or devices represent departures, or *deviations*, from the norm of a competitive market economy. By narrowing opportunities and weakening competitive pressures, they limit the scope and incentive for businesses to perform their primary role. In so far as higher profits are earned as a direct result of such deviations, even a single cheer would be excessive. On the other hand, in so far as governments withhold, pare down or get rid of dubious forms of special treatment for businesses (and for others too), they extend the scope and improve the functioning of markets; and the effect of this is to make profitability a better indicator of the contribution that enterprises make to the welfare of people in general.

Alongside anti-competitive deviations, a further influence which may impair the signalling function of profits, and which itself often arises from attempts to deal with externalities, is *over-regulation*. The pre-1960s Australian ban on iron ore exports is a good instance. On the one hand, it denied to mining firms an opportunity to make investments that could prove, and in the event did prove, worthwhile. At the same time, though less visibly, it restricted competitive pressures on businesses more generally. If the ban had been maintained, the Pilbara developments could not have taken place. As a result, the output of some other goods and services within the Australian economy would now be greater than it is. Although no one can say just which activities have been squeezed out at the margin, such has been an effect of this as of any other successful new venture: market competition is not just between close substitutes, but has a system-wide aspect. The more closely an economy is regulated, the greater the risk that the primary role of business will be less effectively performed because both opportunities and competitive pressures have been curtailed.

This general conclusion applies even where the purpose of regulation is clear and universally accepted, as in the case of health and safety provisions. There is an ever-present risk that progress will be identified too closely with stricter and more uniform standards and the prohibitions that often go with them. A leading instance of such over-zealous attitudes is the adoption across the world of the 'precautionary principle' as a guide to conduct, legal rulings and official regulation. In the name of this innocent-sounding formula, standards can be imposed at arbitrary levels, on the basis of alarmist intuitions as to what might occur, with little regard either for scientific evidence or for the likely resulting effects on costs and benefits at the margin.[4] More specifically, a recent example of what appears to be over-regulation is the proposed new regime for the regulation of chemicals within the European Union, as set out in 2003 by the European Commission. Here is one summary, from a scientific source and not from the chemicals firms affected, of what the initial proposals of the Commission involved: 'The legislation is impractical and has enormous economic and ethical implications. It suggests extensive safety testing of all previously untested chemicals manufactured in quantities of over one tonne, irrespective of likely risk, including such compounds as common salt and sodium bicarbonate.'[5] In such cases, there is a strong possibility that the costs which regulation imposes at the margin on people in general will exceed the value of the benefits to them. There is of course a place for regulation of economic behaviour, and there is ample room for debate

---

4   The case against reliance on the principle is set out in Julian Morris, *Rethinking Risk and the Precautionary Principle*, Butterworth-Heinemann, Oxford, 2000.

5   From a letter to *The Times*, 31 July 2003, from Professor Colin Blakemore, president of the (British) Biosciences Federation.

as to what form it should take and how strict it should be. The point is that regulation has the potential to worsen, as well as to improve, the signalling function of profits.

Within this economic approach, therefore, one of the tasks of economic policy is to harness profit-oriented enterprises more closely to the general welfare, by trying to find suitable ways to deal with externalities and 'market failure', through action to reduce deviations, and by improving the design of regulations and regulatory systems. In carrying out these tasks, the profit motive itself, and the enterprise (or 'capitalist') system with it, are left intact and unquestioned. The object is not to 'give capitalism a human face', but to ensure that the primary role of business is more effectively performed.

Of course, economic policy has other aspects and dimensions. In relation to the general welfare, governments are continuously involved with issues of monetary stability, public finance and international trade and payments. Moreover, they and those they represent are deeply concerned, not only with the welfare of people in general, but also with questions of distribution, equity and fairness: these enter into virtually the whole range of actions and decisions. Within the economic approach, all these various aims are acknowledged; but all of them are viewed as the concern of governments and not of enterprises. Businesses are neither required nor expected to adopt or to further them.

Four features of the economic approach thus described are worth noting. First, and as just remarked, it is for governments rather than business enterprises to define objectives, and to design policies and give effect to them. Businesses and other outside agencies may be consulted, but they do not share responsibility. Profit contamination, along with other aspects and dimensions of economic policy, is for governments to deal with, not corporations. Second, the perspective is economy-wide, and the focus is on the primary role of business. Enterprises themselves are treated as reactive: they appear as little more than units, faceless entities that respond to the stimulus of profit opportunities and the threat of losses, with benefit to others besides themselves. Little or no attention is paid to the business state of mind – the attitudes, motives, values, ideals and aspirations of profit-oriented enterprises and those who own, lead or manage them. Third, the approach is timeless and universal: it implicitly rejects the notion that a new era has just dawned. There is no suggestion that the issues and problems posed by externalities, deviations and over-regulation have undergone fundamental changes in recent years, still less that (to quote the dust jacket of *Walking the Talk*) 'the business of business has changed'. Fourth, no reference is made to social pressures such as those just described in Chapter 4.

How far these features undermine the economic approach, or limit its usefulness, can best be judged by contrasting it with the way in which the same issue, of the relationship between profitability and the general welfare, is treated in today's doctrine of CSR.

Sustainable development and profits: the CSR approach

In one respect, namely the treatment of externalities relating to the environment, there is some common ground. In many presentations of the case for CSR, though not all, emphasis is given to the environmental role of prices and markets and to ways in which this role could be made more effective. For example, the dust jacket text of *Walking the Talk* lays down the principle that 'markets must be mobilized in favor of sustainability'. In the book itself, a chapter is devoted to 'The market' and another to 'The right framework'; and in both chapters there are references to the need for many currently prevailing prices to be adjusted, so as 'to ensure that markets begin to reflect ecological truths' (p. 68). There is room for argument as to what constitutes ecological truth, and whether markets have yet to begin to reflect it. But in so far as CSR advocates regard governments, rather than businesses, as responsible for 'mobilising markets', the line of thinking here is much the same as in the economic approach. Profits are to be made a better indicator through reform of official policies. One source of 'profit contamination' is recognised as such.

Despite this overlap, however, the CSR approach is radically different. For one thing, it typically places little emphasis on the second source of profit contamination, namely, deviations from the competitive norm. Indeed, as will be seen, it points towards further restrictions on economic freedom. Again, and as will also appear, it puts in question or rejects the four features of the economic approach that were listed above. But the fundamental difference is that the CSR approach views the leading task of policy, and the contribution to it of businesses, from an altogether different viewpoint. Except incidentally, it is not concerned with ways of making profits a better guide. Instead, it offers a rival criterion for judging, valuing and directing business activities.

In the economic approach as outlined above, profitability is a guiding light, and a valid *goal* for businesses, because of its links to the general welfare; and the links can be improved, and its status as a business goal thus made more legitimate from a wider viewpoint, through actions by governments to extend the scope of competitive markets and to make good their limitations.

By contrast, the doctrine of CSR sets sustainable development as a universally accepted goal that businesses should pursue, and views higher profitability as the expected *result* of pursuing it. To quote the president of the WBCSD, Bjørn Stigson, in his foreword to *Walking the Talk* (p. 8), the object of WBCSD members is to 'run their companies in the best interests of human society and the natural environment, now and in the future'; and 'companies can do themselves good through doing right for society at large and the environment'. In the CSR approach, therefore, profits are not taken as a *criterion*, as an indicator of an enterprise's contribution to the general welfare. Instead, they are viewed as the *reward* of virtuous conduct, which itself will promote the general welfare directly. By embracing CSR and virtuous conduct, companies will serve the public interest; and in the course of time they can be expected to make higher profits by doing so.

In this way of thinking, it is taken for granted that what is involved in businesses 'doing right for society at large and the environment' is known and agreed. Advocates of CSR speak and write as though there were a well-marked and universally approved path of virtue and enlightened self-interest, following the trail of sustainable development, which all businesses can recognise and take if only they choose to do so. The actions that they should adopt in consequence, which are likewise well defined and generally agreed, are reflected in 'society's expectations' of them.

These actions go well beyond legal obligations. The treatment of externalities is a case in point. Within the economic approach, it is for governments, albeit with outside advice and consultation, to decide which externalities are genuine and significant and what measures should be taken to deal with them. Today as in the past, the duty of businesses is to operate within the framework thus set:

the respective roles and relationships of business and government are seen as being unchanged by recent events. The CSR approach, by contrast, reflects the idea that a new era has now dawned, in which enlightened businesses have to act as innovators and pace-setters. For example, they should be ready, following similarly enlightened public opinion, to judge for themselves the set of prices that would best 'reflect the worth of the earth', and conduct their operations as though these 'shadow' prices were real or about to become so. This gives a new meaning to the notion of 'internal-ising externalities', and places new responsibilities on businesses.

It is not only externalities which are involved. On the dust jacket of *Walking the Talk* reference is made to 'the vanguard who have developed leading-edge environmental and social institu-tions'. In the name of sustainable development, these vanguard businesses have to endorse broader objectives, and new lines of action both for themselves and for those they have dealings with. The extended responsibilities thus proposed chiefly come under the headings of 'environmental' and 'social'. Some indications of what they include can be found in *Walking the Talk*:

- 'The basic business contribution to sustainable development ... is *eco-efficiency...*' (p. 83). 'Stepping up efforts in eco-efficiency will require a new contract among society [*sic*], government and business. Under such a contract, corporate leaders would pledge to invest in eco-efficient innovation – that is, to achieve radical rather than incremental environmental improvement over the long term, to work to reduce global inequalities, and to be responsible employers and community members' (p. 84).
- 'In a changing global arena, the social aspects of business

are taking on a more business-focused meaning – whether in the form of ethical trade, social accountability, community investment, or good labor practice' (p. 107).

- '… sustainable development is partly about social justice' (p. 12).

In fact, the proposed new range of objectives and concerns goes wider than these quotations might suggest. For many companies, the 'social' dimension of the 'triple bottom line' is seen as covering such issues as (1) the enforcement and extension of human rights and 'core standards', and (2) adoption of the goal of 'diversity' in relation to company policies and practices relating to recruitment, selection and promotion.

Within this approach, the relevant conception of the general welfare – that is, the conception that bears on the role and conduct of businesses – is greatly extended. In the economic approach outlined above, it is defined with reference to what people show themselves, or would show themselves, willing to pay for. That there may be other values, other criteria than willingness to pay, is not denied. Rather, the assumption is implicitly made that these other aspects, and the other objectives which people and governments may have endorsed, are not pertinent to judging business performance. In today's rival approach, this assumption is rejected. Given the broad interpretation of sustainable development which has taken hold, the conception of the general welfare that is relevant to business is held to cover human rights, social justice, the plight of poor countries, discrimination and equal opportunities, 'social exclusion', the treatment of local communities and indigenous peoples, and stakeholder engagement, as well as 'radical environmental improvement'. Business performance is to be assessed, and so far as possible measured, in relation to all of these. In consequence, the vanguard companies, and those who later follow in their footsteps, have to embark on (to quote the formula used on p. 126 of *Walking the Talk*) a 'sustainable transformation'.

What are the reasons for thinking that the world has recently changed in ways that point to the need for such a transformation? Why is it that the diverse objectives and concerns listed above have *only now* emerged as the right and proper agenda of responsible businesses? As seen already, the main answer of the authors of *Walking the Talk* is that a new era has dawned, because globalisation has come upon the world. They also argue (p. 60) that: 'During the 1990s a number of new social and development issues moved quickly up the business agenda – new views of corporate social responsibility, the need to address the developmental needs of the South, and the question of how to tackle the gap between the "haves" and the "have-nots"'. But as noted in Chapter 3 above, such arguments do not hold water. No such dawning has occurred. The 'developmental needs of the South', and the differences between rich and poor, are not problems that have newly emerged; and the implication that the progress of poor countries now depends, as never before, on the conscious efforts of business enterprises to promote it is contradicted by past and current evidence. Recent moves towards greater freedom of international trade and capital flows, and other developments such as privatisation, have neither put in question the primary role of business nor established a case for redefining the goals and conduct of enterprises. Governments have neither lost nor surrendered power to MNEs, nor is there a newly created power deficit across the world which responsible businesses should join in making good. In the

1990s as in the past, closer international economic integration has not brought with it the dramatic consequences that are assumed, with little by way of argument or reference to facts, by these and other authors.

However, a case can be made that this is not the whole story. A possible fallback position for proponents of CSR is that, even though their approach is typically linked to a distorted view of what globalisation has brought, it can nevertheless be stated in a modified and more acceptable form. The modified argument would be that the conscious pursuit of sustainable development by businesses today is desirable for other and more solid reasons, which go well beyond the possible effects of recent globalisation: it is not so much that a new era has dawned, but that a good idea has now come into its own. Even in this modified version, the approach could still point to the need for a 'transformation' in the aims and conduct of businesses. The purpose of the transformation would be to take account of concerns that are widely shared, and which have both spread and intensified in recent years, relating to environmental damage or threats and various forms of inequality, both national and international.

In any case, the social pressures described in the previous chapter are real. If public opinion, official as well as unofficial, is wedded or reconciled to global salvationist ideas, and favours the adoption of CSR, should businesses not respond accordingly – the more so if, as the CSR supporters maintain, this will in fact serve the interests of long-term profitability? To consider this question, and to assess the case for some version of the CSR approach, it is necessary to consider the likely consequences of adopting it – for profits, the welfare of people in general, and the ways in which the two are connected.

Enterprise choices, profitability and the general welfare

Giving effect to CSR, in the name of sustainable development, is liable to affect both enterprise profitability and the general welfare: the two aspects need to be kept distinct. Under both headings, there may be negative and positive effects to be taken into account. Where the balance lies will depend to a large extent on how far the CSR approach is taken up by businesses everywhere, as its advocates would wish, rather than just by vanguard firms.

To begin with the negative side, it is clear that, within enterprises themselves, a genuine commitment to CSR carries with it obvious dangers of raising costs and impairing efficient operation, and hence, other things being equal, reducing prospective profitability: *to adopt the role of vanguard firm is not a riskless decision*. If this were not so, if there were no question of trade-offs and hard choices, the whole notion of CSR would be unimportant if not trivial. Three main sources of enterprise risk can be identified. All of them are ignored or played down in typical statements of the case for CSR.

One source of risk relates to the agenda and performance of management. Taking the path of CSR brings with it an extension of managerial tasks and responsibilities to take greater account of a range of environmental and 'social' concerns. To take a recent British example, the retailer Marks & Spencer has committed itself to running 'an extensive work experience scheme for the disadvantaged', covering homeless people, disadvantaged schoolchildren, lone parents, and first-generation students from non-academic backgrounds (*Financial Times*, 4 February 2004). Besides adding directly to enterprise costs, such concerns are additional to the basic – and highly demanding – tasks associated with meeting the wishes and orders of customers while identifying, and responding to, opportunities to innovate and to bring down costs. Alongside and linked to this dilution of attention and energies, directors and managers are called on to involve themselves, as part of 'multiple stakeholder engagement', in time-consuming consultations, negotiations and review processes with an array of outside groups. In *Walking the Talk*, stakeholders are said (p. 150) to 'range through' 'employees, shareholders, communities, NGOs, consumers, suppliers, partners, governments, and society at large', while the European Commission, in its 2001 Green Paper on CSR, defines 'stakeholder', comprehensively, as referring to 'any individual, community or organisation that affects, or is affected by, the operations of a company'. Many of the groups thus listed are unconcerned with the commercial success of firms, while some of them are deeply hostile to private business and capitalism as such. Even for those that are relatively well disposed towards profit-oriented business, their closer involvement in its affairs is not a costless matter for an enterprise. It is true that for many businesses today new and wider forms of engagement may be hard to avoid. The point is, however, that the doctrine of CSR treats them as purely advantageous and as a sign of virtue.

A second source of risk is that CSR involves developing new systems for recording, monitoring, reporting on and evaluating the firm's performance in relation to a range of environmental and social goals. To design and operate such systems adds directly to costs, as well as taking up managerial time and effort.

Third, the adoption of more exacting self-chosen environmental and social norms and standards to govern the conduct of business operations is itself liable to add to costs, possibly substantially. The effect is magnified if, as the doctrine of CSR requires, firms insist on the observance of these same standards by their partners, suppliers and contractors – and even, as some would argue, their customers.

These various negative impacts on the performance of enterprises are directly and unavoidably passed on to their shareholders and customers. In so far as CSR makes managers less effective in performing their basic tasks, and gives rise to higher operating costs, the effect is to make people in general poorer.

What of the positive side? From an enterprise viewpoint, the three risks to profitability can be viewed as acceptable if they bring with them countervailing financial gains which will tip the balance, so as to yield a positive net result. Such enterprise gains may arise from better motivation of employees, and wider choice of recruits, because of the firm's commitment to CSR; a preference on the part of investors and fund managers for investing in firms that are seen to be socially responsible; and – probably the most important factor – customer preferences for buying from such firms. As noted, the advocates of CSR believe that a positive net outcome is to be expected, in the longer term if not immediately.

For any single business, much may depend on what others do. In so far as the costs and performance of vanguard firms are adversely affected by any or all of the three sources of enterprise risk, without fully offsetting gains, they are liable to lose ground to their less venturesome competitors. On the other hand, if these other firms soon fall in behind the vanguard, by taking the path of CSR themselves, such competitive threats are eliminated or greatly reduced. When it comes to the general welfare, however, the net effects of conformity are not necessarily positive, and could well be negative. In so far as the results of adopting the CSR approach are to weaken enterprise performance, and hence to make people in general worse off, they will be magnified in so far as businesses generally, and not just the vanguard firms, take this course.

A key question, therefore, concerns the economy-wide impact of CSR, as distinct from its effects on enterprise profitability: is the widespread or universal adoption of the doctrine likely to generate net benefits for people in general? As noted, the supporters of CSR are in no doubt about this. They believe that the path of virtue is well marked out, and that what they see as 'doing right by society at large and the environment' is bound to make the world a better place. But such an outcome is not to be taken for granted. It is not clear that the actions now prescribed for firms in the name of corporate citizenship or sustainable development would in fact yield genuine and substantial benefits to the public at large, *or even that their effects would on balance be positive*. Still less can it be assumed that these net effects would be, not only positive in themselves, but large enough to outweigh the costs that are liable to arise from the three sources of enterprise risk identified above.

A relevant issue here concerns the status and validity of the various wider enterprise goals and practices which are laid down in CSR doctrine, in the name of sustainable development, and which do not directly contribute to profits. By definition, these are voluntarily chosen and set by enterprises themselves. This poses a question as to how far businesses have the right or the competence to make such determinations. It is true that, as noted in the previous chapter, public opinion, in OECD countries at any rate, has now given broad approval to the idea that businesses should consciously aim to promote sustainable development. But this is a different matter from enterprises themselves deciding just how to interpret the notion, by endorsing their own goals and targets under such headings as 'eco-efficiency', 'ethical trade' and 'social justice'. What is the authority for such targets, or indeed for the headings themselves, given that they are not prescribed by law?

The advocates of CSR have a standard twofold response to this question. They argue that these various social and environmental goals, and the actions taken by firms in pursuit of them, respond to society's expectations. Further, they assume, or at any rate do not question, that these expectations accurately mirror the public interest, so that by complying with them businesses would unquestionably improve the state of the world. Both these lines of argument, however, are open to question.

First, it has to be asked to what extent the demands on businesses in the name of CSR, and the hostility to companies and profit-making that often go with them, actually reflect public opinion. Pro-CSR businesses and business organisations have typically identified society's expectations with the current demands of NGOs, 'ethical' investment funds and other radical critics of the market economy; but how far these interests are representative of people in general is debatable. In any case, not all public expectations, and the pressures on businesses that arise from them, are reasonable and well founded. Where they are not, businesses and business organisations have a right, and arguably a duty, to question the arguments that are brought to bear by their critics, to resist the pressures, and to make a case, on public interest grounds, for wiser courses of action.

Second, it is not to be taken for granted that the actions undertaken by businesses to meet self-chosen environmental and social goals, even if they meet expectations that are widely held and serve to appease critics, will on balance increase the general welfare: they could well do more harm than good. There is a clear risk that, in the name of CSR and in pursuit of questionable objectives which they have defined for themselves, businesses will contribute on their own account to the further over-regulation of economic life.

Such dangers may arise in connection with both environmental and social policies. More exacting enterprise-imposed environmental standards may not bring net gains in welfare: at the margin, the additional costs to people in general may outweigh the benefits to them. Further, and as noted in Chapter 3 above, the principle of uniform norms and standards, whether environmental or social, is open to serious objection where local circumstances are widely different, and hence, most notably, where different countries are involved. Insistence on common company-wide practice may narrow the scope for mutually beneficial market-based transactions, many of which would serve especially the interests of poor people. Under both headings, environmental and social, market opportunities may be curtailed and competitive pressures weakened.

Over-regulation may also result from the policies and programmes which some companies have introduced to promote 'diversity', in the name of social justice as they interpret the notion: a leading instance, referred to in Chapter 4 of *Misguided Virtue*, is that of Shell. In so far as such actions result in company-wide policies which limit the scope for free and independent choice in hiring, recruitment, selection, promotion, dismissals and terms and conditions of employment, the risk arises that they will restrict both managerial initiative and freedom of contract in ways that will not only add to enterprise costs but deprive ordinary people of opportunities to make themselves better off. A whole range of mutually advantageous deals, contracts and working arrangements may be precluded.

To sum up: it is questionable whether expressed broad concerns of governments and public opinion about environmental issues, and in relation to equality and fairness, should be reflected in the aims and conduct of enterprises if not embodied in laws and regulations. Businesses cannot ignore the pressures that are brought to bear on them under these headings, but they are not obliged to treat all of them as reasonable and well founded. Moreover, the actions that enterprises take in response to such pressures may do more harm than good, and are liable to make them less effective in the performance of their primary role. These effects remain even if such actions have a positive net effect on profitability: the two aspects are not the same, and the signalling function of profits is impaired if enterprises have to act in ways that reduce welfare because otherwise they would suffer financially.

Such an argument does not at all imply that businesses should be prevented from taking steps, on their own initiative and commercial judgement, to develop 'leading-edge environmental and social institutions' and the codes, policies and practices that go with them. Within a competitive market economy, they can choose for themselves, in the light of their own particular circumstances and within the limits set by law, how far to go in this direction, and in what ways. Whether or not to sign on to CSR is for them to decide. Provided that each business is free to map out its own course, and its customers are likewise free to decide for themselves how to spend their money, there might be little cause for concern if CSR proved to be a popular choice. Its adoption by individual companies could be viewed as a legitimate competitive strategy, embarked on in the expectation that people would be attracted by the idea of buying from, investing in or working for a vanguard business.

By the same token, however, the possibility ought to exist and to be kept open, as one of the elements that go to make up a competitive market economy, for enterprises that take a different view of their situation, interests and responsibilities to decide against joining the vanguard, or to desert from its ranks. In so far as they are denied the freedom to make such choices, because the adoption of CSR has become legally or effectively binding, competitive pressures will be reduced, market opportunities narrowed, and business performance of its primary role impaired.

Undermining the market economy

Social pressures to bring about such restrictions on economic freedom can come from various sources, and the most insistent of these could be the vanguard firms themselves. In so far as 'socially responsible' businesses find that their new role is bringing with it higher costs and less effective managerial performance, for any or all of the reasons sketched out above, and that profitability is suffering as a result, they have a strong interest in ensuring that their unregenerate rivals are induced or compelled to follow suit. To quote the authors of *Walking the Talk* (p. 19), 'smart CEOs not only are going to orient their companies toward sustainability, but also are going to try to orient society toward sustainability', and (p. 62) 'The goal must be to encourage whole market segments to change so that supportive companies are not doomed to unfair competitive disadvantage'.

One means of bringing nonconformists into line is through the pressure of public opinion, including in particular the NGOs. In effect, and as noted already, many large businesses have now chosen to ally themselves with what they see as relatively moderate

NGOs, whether from motives of prudence or because of shared opinions and objectives. In this connection, it is worth quoting again the story told some time ago in a speech by Hugh Morgan, who at the time was head of the Australian mining company WMC Resources. He spoke of a then recent conversation with the CEO of 'a very large resources-based corporation' who had said to him: 'Hugh, don't you understand? My organisation is run by Greenpeace today, and it is my job to ensure that Greenpeace is running yours tomorrow'. Behind this chilling pleasantry lies an all too real possibility of anti-competitive pressures being brought to bear on nonconforming firms, through campaigns in which vanguard companies and NGOs have joined forces, often with moral support from government departments and international agencies.[6]

However, the most effective way of ensuring that vanguard firms do not suffer adverse commercial consequences from their socially responsible actions is through securing official directives or regulations to make such actions binding on all. In so far as governments induce or compel businesses to have regard or give effect to the doctrine of CSR, the path of virtue will be smoothed and vanguard firms bailed out. Such official impositions and obligations can be presented as ensuring 'a level playing field'.

Two lines of action are open to governments that wish to move in this direction. One is to require that businesses should recognise, and have regard to, ethical, environmental and social considerations. Several member governments within the European

---

6   The NGO thus commended by Morgan's CEO acquaintance, Greenpeace, issued in 2002 a leaflet, designed to enlist new supporters, for which the title was 'Get your filthy hands off my future'. The hands in question are those of unregenerate businesses and 'governments which tolerate their actions'.

Union, including France, Germany and the UK, have in fact passed laws prescribing that pension funds should take these considerations into account in making their investment choices. A second and more far-reaching course would be to translate into laws or regulations, or near-mandatory official guidelines and codes of conduct, the policies and practices that conformity to CSR is taken to require. While this latter stage does not appear to have been reached in any country as yet, it has now become a serious possibility, at any rate in the European Union. Such binding provisions could be imposed through international agencies, with the approval or acquiescence of their member states, as well as by national governments acting individually or in concert.

Alongside these general prescriptive actions, governments can also be asked to help the cause of CSR, or may volunteer their assistance unasked, in more specific ways. One form of official support would be to give preferences in awarding public contracts to firms that have signed up to sustainable development and CSR: such a suggestion was made in all seriousness not long ago, in a report by a group of European businesses.[7] Again, firms that have embarked on 'environmentally friendly' investments, for example in the supply of renewable energy, can lobby for official action by way of subsidies for these or penalties on rival products. The vanguard companies, to quote again from *Walking the Talk* (p. 154), 'can build strategic alliances with some NGOs and other partners to begin shaping political agendas and markets in such a

---

7   The report was entitled *For an Entrepreneurial and Inclusive Europe*, and was jointly prepared, as a 'business leaders' input' to the Lisbon European Summit meeting of 2000, by a business organisation now known as CSR Europe together with the Copenhagen Centre. In Chapter 5 of *Misguided Virtue* I describe it, for reasons given there, as 'not a responsible document'.

way that these agendas and markets support and reward companies investing in more sustainable technologies, products, and services'. Such an approach provides ample scope for creating new deviations from the competitive norm, possibly under the cloak of correcting for externalities.

Which are the most promising candidates for the role of vanguard firms, and hence the ones that would benefit most from anti-competitive campaigns, restrictive legislation and special favours from governments? It is the large firms, and in particular MNEs based in rich countries, which are cast for the role. These are the businesses that are chiefly under pressure or attack from NGOs and others, and are most subject to scrutiny. They, more than small or purely national businesses, are in the firing line. At the same time, it is these companies which can cope best with tighter and more complex regulations, and are better placed to lobby for official concessions and support. As compared with other enterprises, they have closer contacts with governments; and their more elaborate staffing, with many of the relevant executives increasingly interchangeable with their global salvationist counterparts in consulting firms, government departments, international agencies and NGOs, makes it easier for them to interpret and respond to the demands of CSR. Many of these companies have a clear interest in ensuring that, as social pressures on them become stronger and are reflected in management attitudes, and their own practices are adapted accordingly, smaller, less prominent and more commercially oriented businesses do not escape the net. Similarly, firms based in rich countries have an incentive to see to it that their competitors in developing countries are made subject to the same pressures, and the same regulations, that bear on them. Many of today's demands for CSR are prompted by hostility, largely or entirely unwarranted, to the leading MNEs. Ironically, however, these are the very businesses that may stand to gain most from its general adoption or imposition, because this could weaken the competitive pressures on them.

It is the possible economy-wide effects of CSR which are especially worrying. While actions by individual businesses to give effect to it may well do more harm than good, this may not be a matter for much concern provided that both they and other firms are free to determine their goals and strategies, and to reappraise and change them at will. Conversely, the risk that people in general will be made worse off in the name of corporate virtue is much increased in so far as businesses everywhere are made to toe the line, whether by social pressures, official or unofficial, or more formally through laws or regulations. If across the world firms are increasingly obliged to practise 'multiple stakeholder engagement', to institute 'triple bottom line' accounting and reporting systems, to pursue 'radical environmental improvement', to embrace 'diversity' and 'social justice' in their human resources policies, to adopt more exacting and more uniform environmental and social norms and standards in all the locations where they operate, and to enforce those standards on the other businesses they have dealings with, market opportunities will be closed off and competitive pressures reduced. In so far as governments lend an additional hand through giving special favours to practitioners of CSR, new distortions will be created and the market economy further undermined. That all these actions can be viewed and presented as furthering the cause of sustainable development does not detract from their damaging effects on rich and poor alike.

Such a trend towards a more regulated world, with social pressures serving to weaken competitive pressures, would cause the primary role of business to be less well performed; and *this effect would remain whether or not the consequences of taking the path of CSR for the profitability of particular enterprises proved to be, on balance, favourable.* The case against the general adoption of CSR by businesses, in the name of sustainable development, is not that it would necessarily be bad for enterprise profits, but that it would reduce welfare.

In so far as the carrying into effect of CSR brings with it new forms of over-regulation and further deviations from the competitive norm, it would actually make profitability a worse indicator of an enterprise's contribution to the general welfare: *it is itself a potential source of 'profit contamination'.* Within a well-functioning market economy, by contrast, profits may fully deserve two cheers.

Motives, morality and outcomes[8]

This latter notion is not a popular one: that a market economy brings with it close links between profitability and the general welfare is not accepted doctrine. Now as in the past, profits are often viewed with suspicion; and indeed, such suspicions help to explain the widespread support for CSR. Why is the positive role of profitability so little appreciated, and the profit motive so widely questioned or condemned?

One influential reason, truly a poor one, is that the pursuit of profits is seen as arising from greed, and hence as reflecting a deeply unworthy motive, if not one of the seven deadly sins. Profits

8   Some of the issues raised in this section are considered in a recent volume of essays entitled *Economy and Virtue: Essays on the Theme of Markets and Morality*, edited by Dennis O'Keeffe, Institute of Economic Affairs, London, 2004.

are taken to be the reward of conduct which is at best amoral and at worst anti-social. In this caricature of reality, the positive role of profits as an indicator of net social benefit, and the signalling function that goes with it, have no place. The focus is on motives only, and these are both caricatured and misconstrued. It is of course true that the search for profits, and the wish to avoid losses, reflects the interests of a business and those who direct it. But the opponents of business typically make no distinction between self-interest, on the one hand, and on the other selfishness, materialism, egotism and greed. The one is not at all to be identified with the others. Indeed, as Adam Smith pointed out some 250 years ago, in his *Theory of Moral Sentiments*, the pursuit of self-interest typically goes together with what are rightly prized as forms of virtuous conduct: 'The habits of economy, industry, discretion, attention and application of thought are generally supposed to be cultivated from self-interested motives, and at the same time are apprehended to be very praiseworthy qualities which deserve the esteem and approbation of everybody'.[9] In any case, the motivation of entrepreneurially minded businesspersons clearly goes well beyond the acquisitive pursuit of riches for their own sake, though personal wealth and status may of course be part of what they, like many other people, hope to achieve.

A more moderate criticism of the role of profits, which likewise focuses on motives, is that the conduct of business is typically not founded on the desire and intention to do good works, simply because it is indelibly tainted with self-interest. A classic comment on this preoccupation with the worthiness of enterprise

---

9   Adam Smith, *The Theory of Moral Sentiments*, Liberty Fund, Indianopolis, IN, [1759] 1982, p. 304.

motives was made, also by Adam Smith, in *The Wealth of Nations*. Justly famous though it is, the quotation is worth another airing. It is through bargaining, says Smith, '… that we obtain from one another the far greater part of those good offices that we stand in need of. It is not from the benevolence of the butcher, the brewer, or the baker, that we expect our dinner, but from their regard to their own interest.'[10] Smith's brilliant observation applies today, and indeed it can be put more strongly, since it can be extended to cover the dynamic aspect of business activity. It is not only from being able to rely on the timely routine provision of everyday commodities that ordinary people – as also public agencies and businesses themselves – benefit from 'regard to their own interest' on the part of enterprises: they also gain from the development of new and improved products and services and the introduction of cost-reducing innovations. Provided that, and in so far as, the regard of individuals and enterprises for their own interest finds expression in anticipating, meeting and even helping to shape the wishes of those who buy from them, and doing these things in a lawful, resourceful and innovative way, the general welfare is served. This is what a competitive market economy makes possible. For reasons sketched out in Chapter 2 above, such an economy has to be 'capitalist', in the sense that the general run of enterprises within it are privately owned and profit-oriented.

Those who cast doubt on the profit motive and the criterion of profitability rarely make the vital distinction between profits that are performance-related and those that are not: their criticism extends, indiscriminately, to profits as such. In viewing and

---

10 Adam Smith, *The Wealth of Nations*, Liberty Fund, Indianapolis, IN, [1776] 1981, pp. 26–7.

judging business enterprises and the role of business, people who think in this way fall into two related errors of perception. First, they pay too much attention to motives rather than results; and second, they assume that good results can flow only from virtuous conduct, the aim of which is to confer benefits on others, and which must necessarily involve some element of personal sacrifice. Hence the whole notion of acting from self-interest is disparaged or viewed with suspicion.

These attitudes go together with a failure to recognise the range of purposes which a competitive market economy serves. As Samuel Brittan has noted:

> An economic system has at least five functions
>
> 1 co-ordinate the activity of millions of individuals, households and firms;
> 2 obtain information about people's desires, tastes and preferences;
> 3 decide which productive techniques to use;
> 4 promote new ideas, tastes and activities which people would not have thought of without entrepreneurial initiative;
> 5 create incentives for people to act on such information.
>
> Only the fifth, incentive, function of markets could be abandoned in a community of saints. The others would still be required for the saints to know how best to serve their fellows.[11]

---

11 The quotation is from p. 11 of *Essays, Moral, Political and Economic*, published by the Edinburgh University Press for the David Hume Institute, 1998. Brittan's final observation finds a recent echo in an essay by Israel Kirzner, in the book referred to above, *Economy and Virtue*. Kirzner notes (p. 91) that 'the coordinative properties of free markets would be as fully relevant for societies of saintly market participants as for ruthlessly selfish and materialistic participants'.

All of these functions depend on the role of profits as a signalling device, which the focus on motivation and virtuous conduct obscures or disregards.

Does this mean that the notion of virtuous conduct has no place in the conduct of business enterprises? Not at all. Running a business, like other forms of human conduct, has a moral dimension. Today as always, business enterprises, and those in charge of them, have moral as well as legal obligations. Situations can well arise in which directors and managers, and often shareholders too, may need to consider what it is right for a company to do, as well as what is legally permitted to it or required of it. This is liable to happen even in countries that have well-functioning legal systems and governments. Where the legal framework is weak, or governments are corrupt, authoritarian or ineffective, the need for companies to make their own considered assessments is correspondingly greater.

Considerations of prudence are also relevant here. Now more than ever, businesses are under pressure to answer their critics and to justify what they do. The larger firms in particular have to be continuously concerned with their public reputation. They have to show that they treat people fairly and humanely, that their activities are not giving rise to damaging external effects and that, where current environmental and social concerns appear to them well founded, they are ready to contribute, in ways that are consistent with their primary purpose and obligations as commercial entities, to common efforts to deal with these.

Not only do business enterprises as such have moral as well as legal obligations, but so also, as individuals, do those who in their various professional capacities influence, direct and manage enterprise affairs. In the corporate world of today, as Martin

Wolf has pointed out: 'Corporate managers are trustees. So are fund managers. The more they view themselves (and are viewed) as such, the less likely they are to exploit opportunities created by the conflicts of interest within a business' (*Why Globalization Works*, p. 50). Issues of professional ethics and integrity are inseparable from the conduct of business operations, as they are in other spheres such as law or medicine or education. To take them seriously does not mean setting aside commercial responsibilities, *which themselves impose professional and moral obligations.* The search for profit is fully compatible with professionalism, humanity, and the wish to act honourably.

Issues of business morality and motivation, though often connected, are not to be seen as identical. It is too simple, in business affairs as elsewhere, to think in terms of a clear and stark alternative between self-interested behaviour, on the one hand, and on the other, conscious conformity to ethical principles. The everyday goals, concerns and ambitions of business leaders and managers, as of other professionals, may have little direct reference to either. As G. L. S. Shackle has noted in the quotation that appears on the half-title verso, business is creative. Those engaged in it may be chiefly driven by the satisfaction and excitement of meeting new challenges and coping successfully with demanding technical and organisational problems. They are also concerned to stand well with their peers, employees, neighbours and families, as well as their customers. Work satisfaction, and personal and professional reputation and pride, provide motives which, though neither disinterested nor altruistic, go beyond both enterprise profit and personal financial gain. Indeed, in the absence of such a range of motives and concerns the primary role of business would be less effectively performed. As in the case of Lang Hancock, quoted in the opening paragraph of this chapter, the entrepreneurial qualities that chiefly count may be 'vision, comprehension and faith'.

At the same time, professional and enterprise motivation, however creative and dedicated, can prove misdirected if the test of profitability is relevant and not met. A good example is the Anglo-French Concorde project, which has recently been brought to an end more than forty years after its inception. Those most closely involved with the development of the Concorde believed, with reason, that they and their organisations were making history. They saw the successful construction, proving and entry into service of the first supersonic civil transport aircraft as bringing about a spectacular technical advance and an array of associated benefits to air travellers everywhere, to the aircraft industries of France and Britain, and to the national economies and international standing of both countries. This vision no doubt gave an extra edge to the professional satisfactions derived from meeting the formidable technical challenges that the programme offered. It might be hard to find a more wholesome set of motives entering into the conduct and completion of a would-be commercial investment project.[12] Yet the end result of the huge expenditures on research, development and production was a true white elephant – a machine which no airline in the world, given a free choice, would have been prepared to accept, operate and maintain even if offered

---

12 Except that, as in most such undertakings, there was both the disposition and the incentive to underestimate the costs and technical difficulties of the project, and to overestimate the prospective gains from it – all the more so because the project was wholly financed by the governments concerned.

to it as a gift. The dominant outcome of the programme was to make people in France and Britain poorer.[13]

Three broad conclusions can be drawn from what has been said under this heading. First, in assessing the usefulness of economic activities and ventures, it is results which count rather than enterprise motives. Second, for goods and services that are or could be marketed, the acid test of results – and one that, as noted earlier, is open to improvement as such by well-chosen public policies – is that of profitability. Third, the fact that businesses and those who run and control them have moral obligations does not put in question self-interested conduct, the primary role of business, or the signalling function of profits in a market economy.

Profits, CSR and the conduct and role of business

On the complex issues of corporate and individual conduct which have to be faced in business, now as in the past, the doctrine of CSR, even when stripped of its false conception of the changes that globalisation has brought, has little of value to contribute.[14] It glosses over, or assumes away, many of the difficult choices and trade-offs that businesses and business leaders have to confront.

13 The Concorde episode forms part of the subject matter of an article of mine published in 1977 as P. D. Henderson, 'Two British Errors', *Oxford Economic Papers*, 1977. The second 'error' in question was the Second UK Nuclear Power Programme.

14 Again, so far as my reading goes, it has nothing useful to say about issues of corporate governance. These are well surveyed in Elaine Sternberg's book, *Corporate Governance: Accountability in the Marketplace*, Institute of Economic Affairs, London, 2nd edn, 2004. Both in this book and in her parallel study of business ethics, *Just Business: Business Ethics in Action*, Oxford University Press, 2nd edn, 2000, Dr Sternberg deals also with issues relating to CSR.

For example, it gives little attention to the ways in which the pursuit of virtuous conduct, through multi-stakeholder engagement and the adoption of new norms and goals, may divert managerial energies and attention from more directly commercial responsibilities. Again, in presuming that the path of enterprise virtue is well defined and beyond dispute, and that following it will lead to both greater social welfare and higher enterprise profitability, it simply evades the issues.

Although CSR is presented as new and path-breaking, much of the thinking that underlies it betrays the age-old pre-economic fixation on the purity of business motives and the related suspicion of profits as such. CSR advocates, like many others before them, see special or even exclusive merit in actions that are directed (in Hayek's words) 'to the deliberate pursuit of known and observable beneficial ends'.[15] In consequence, they are apt to make a wholly misleading disjunction between the profit-oriented activities of a business and its contribution to the public welfare. For example, the authors of *Walking the Talk* quote with approval (p. 114) a maxim coined by BP, in its 1998 statement of business policies entitled *What We Stand For*, that 'A good business should be both competitively successful and a force for good' – as though the two things were unconnected. Again, the WBCSD, in its 1999 report entitled *Corporate Social Responsibility*, states on the opening page that: 'Although the rationale for the very existence of business at law and in other respects is to generate acceptable [*sic*] returns for its shareholders and investors, business and business leaders have, over the centuries, made significant contributions to the societies

15   F. A. Hayek, *The Fatal Conceit: The Errors of Socialism*, Routledge, London, 1988, p. 80.

of which they form part'. In these and other instances, businesses and business organisations have uncritically accepted a view of the world in which no distinction is drawn between profits that are performance-related and those that are not, while the positive and indeed vital function of the former is overlooked or played down. Profits are viewed as a means to higher ends, through providing elbow room for virtuous conduct, rather than as an indicator of a firm's contribution to the general welfare.

In their scheme of things, the advocates of CSR have unwittingly downgraded both the primary role of business and the claim of profit-oriented private businesses to legitimacy and recognition. They see defence of the market economy in terms of making companies more popular and respected, through redefining their mission and changing their practices to accord with what are seen as society's expectations. Such a way of thinking misses the main point. It may well be true, or eventually become true, that firms have to take the path of CSR, in the interests of profitability or even survival, because of social pressures brought to bear on them or formal legal requirements. But in so far as this trend weakens enterprise performance, limits economic freedom and restricts competition, the effect is not only to reduce welfare: *it is to deprive private business of its distinctive virtues and rationale.* It is no accident that the arguments for thus redefining the role and purpose of businesses are similar to those once made for nationalisation and public ownership of enterprises.

Today as in the past, the case for private business rests, not on the commitment by business enterprises to questionable though widely accepted goals, and their willing compliance with social pressures, but on the links between private ownership, competition and economic freedom within a market-directed economy.

The older standard economic approach, as outlined at the beginning of this chapter, provides a better guide to thought and action than the sustainable development approach. It is not through redefining enterprise goals and ways of operating, along the lines now suggested by CSR adherents, that the business contribution to the general welfare can be improved, but rather through actions that fall outside the competence of business but would serve to strengthen its primary role. Such actions form the subject of the chapter that follows.

6 REINFORCING THE PRIMARY ROLE

Liberalisation as a key element

The primary role of business has not changed in recent years, nor have the ways in which it can be maintained and strengthened. Now as in the past, the business contribution to economic progress arises from the combination of opportunities and pressures that a competitive market economy generates; and the opportunities are widened, and the competitive pressures increased, in so far as economies become freer and the scope of markets is extended. Hence a key element in enlarging and strengthening the primary role of business, as always, is economic *liberalisation*.

To reinforce the business role, thus defined, does not mean conferring favours on corporations or deferring to their interests. Liberalisation is not an instrument for furthering business interests, in either intention or effect. Its purpose is not to placate or enrich businesses – which in fact are often opposed to it, with good reason, as contrary to their interests – nor to increase the power of corporations, which it has no tendency to do. Its twin related purposes are, first, to enlarge the domain of economic freedom for people and enterprises alike, and second, to further the material welfare of people in general. From a liberal standpoint, both purposes can be viewed as ends in themselves, while the first is also a means to the second.[1] To be sure, improvements in material welfare may be linked to other influences than the extent of economic freedom, or changes in its extent; but freedom, and hence liberalisation, are positive influences in every situation where the background conditions of public order and stability are realised.

The effects of economic liberalisation extend well beyond the sphere of corporate business enterprises: the gains that it brings to individuals may be direct, through creating wider opportunities for them, whether as consumers or as workers and suppliers of services, as well as indirect as a result of better business performance. There is no reason to expect, still less to assume, that these gains to people in general, whether direct or indirect, will accrue mainly or exclusively to the rich – though much may depend, in this connection, on how particular forms of liberalisation are put into effect and how consistently liberalisation is pursued.

To argue a case for liberalisation today is not to endorse some abstract laissez-faire or libertarian blueprint: it does not imply, as critics are apt to suggest or presume, accepting uncritically the principle of 'leaving it to the market'. It allows for government action to provide what are clearly 'public goods', for official measures and policies designed to cope with genuine external effects, and for forms of regulation that can be justified on public interest grounds. Again, it leaves room, though not unlimited room, for policies that are concerned with the welfare of particular groups, rather than people in general. It points, not to a well-specified, timeless and universal end-state, but to a direction of

1   I use the term 'liberal' in its continental European rather than its American sense. Hence a liberal is taken to be one who emphasises the value of individual freedom, and who accordingly judges arrangements and policies, whether economic or political, primarily with reference to their effects on freedom.

change. In today's context, it implies no more than a belief that, *as compared with the present state of affairs*, extending the sphere of competitive markets would bring significant and widely diffused gains in material welfare, chiefly though by no means only through reinforcing the primary role of business.

Contrary to what is often argued or assumed, the present state of affairs across the world is far from giving expression to liberal norms: in virtually every economy today, there exist large unrealised possibilities for liberalisation. This can be said even of the OECD member countries; and with a few exceptions, it applies still more to the rest of the world. It is true that, over the past 20 to 25 years, a prevailing tendency in economic policies has been for governments to take a more liberal – or less illiberal – course: on balance, most national economies, as also international trade and capital flows, are freer than they were towards the end of the 1970s when the first signs of what became a liberal trend began to appear. But despite what is often now affirmed, by both advocates and opponents of liberalisation, the cause of economic liberalism has by no means triumphed over this recent period: the world has not at all been made subject to a 'neo-liberal hegemony', nor is 'the end of history' in sight. Even today, the ideas of economic liberalism are accepted only by a small minority; and despite the various market-oriented reforms that have been introduced, in a growing number of countries, there is ample scope for further movement in the same direction. Almost everywhere, and especially in developing and transition countries, the primary role of business could be substantially reinforced.[2]

---

2   The evidence for the historical generalisations made in this paragraph is set out in a short book of mine, *The Changing Fortunes of Economic Liberalism*, Institute of Economic Affairs, London, 2nd edn, 2001.

The scope for liberalisation

One obvious means to widening business opportunities and strengthening competitive pressures is for governments, either individually or in concert, to make international trade and investment flows freer.[3] Despite the liberalisation of cross-border transactions that has taken place in the world, not just through recent 'globalisation' but (on balance) over the whole period since the end of World War II, the establishment of a liberal international economic order is still a distant and unlikely prospect. In virtually every country today, the hold of protectionism remains strong. In the OECD member states, this is to be seen in the assistance given (except in Australia and New Zealand) to domestic agriculture; in the still-persisting quantitative restrictions on imports of textiles and clothing; in the continuing resort to anti-dumping actions; in attempts to make trade subject to the acceptance of minimum international labour and environmental norms and standards; in government procurement practices; in a limited and qualified commitment to liberalisation of trade in services; in the continuing and indeed increasing disposition of leading countries to think in terms of bilateral or regional preferential trading arrangements; and in the interventionist attitudes towards foreign direct investment that led to the failure of the MAI. In the rest of the world, with only a few exceptions, trade barriers are higher and foreign direct investment is more tightly controlled, so that the scope for external liberalisation is greater. Everywhere, official trade policies continue to reflect pre-economic mercantilist ways

---

3   There are good arguments for making international migration freer also; but such a possibility raises wider issues, of residence and citizenship, which go beyond the scope of this book. Issues relating to international migration pose serious problems for economic liberals.

of thinking, within which exports appear as a gain to a country, imports as a loss, and trade liberalisation on one's own account as a concession, to be made only in return for similar concessions on the part of other governments. The WTO ministerial meeting in Cancún in September 2003, which ended prematurely and without result, gave further evidence that these unreconstructed mercantilist notions are still dominant.

Domestically, a leading element in the liberalisation of economies has been, and continues to be, privatisation in its various aspects. One aspect is the opening up to private business participation of industries that had been reserved for public enterprises: for example, this has been one of the features of recent economic reforms in India, where the number of such fenced-off industries has been greatly reduced. In many countries a leading aspect has been and still is denationalisation – the transfer to private firms of publicly owned enterprises and assets. Change of ownership is only part of the picture, however: how far it reinforces market opportunities and competitive pressures depends on related decisions of governments. Much hinges on the extent to which the new arrangements provide for freer access and greater competition: in the UK, for instance, the main welfare gains from privatisation of the gas and electricity industries have come from pro-competitive regulation, rather than the change from public to private ownership as such, though this was a necessary first step. Again, liberalisation will be the more effective in so far as foreign firms are allowed to bid for assets on equal terms: this is one aspect of freedom of entry. In many if not most countries, there is still a long way to go in making the transition from public monopolies to fully competitive private provision.

Besides the sale of public enterprises and the establishment of competitive market arrangements in their place, a further area of privatisation is the opening up of public procurement, and the provision of goods and services that are financed from taxation, to competing private businesses. In many countries, a leading opportunity for moving farther in this direction is to be found in the education system, which has been justly described, in a recently published study, as 'one of the last great nationalised industries'.[4] In particular, there is scope across the world for creating new market opportunities and competitive pressures by ensuring, for instance through the introduction of education vouchers, that free schooling is no longer restricted to being largely or entirely a state monopoly.

A related way of extending the sphere of market-based transactions is to replace free or heavily subsidised provision by user charges. Such 'marketisation' creates a state of affairs in which, as with the general run of goods and services, willingness to pay becomes the basis for determining outcomes. Provided that their real incomes do not suffer, buyers are placed in a more advantageous position, because possibilities for choice and competitive provision are opened up. A drawback of free provision, at any rate in the absence of a voucher scheme, is that people are denied the opportunity to give full expression to their wishes and preferences, and to show through actual purchases what the goods and services they receive are worth to them at the margin: the signalling function of prices is suppressed. As a result of this suppression, buyers are likewise deprived of the opportunity which a market provides for them to influence the conduct of suppliers, by

---

4   Alison Wolf, *Does Education Matter? Myths about Education and Economic Growth*, Penguin, London, 2002, p. 219.

backing their wishes and preferences with money. In competitive markets, as Israel Kirzner has noted,[5] producers can gain only by putting themselves at the service of consumers. For all consumers – whether individuals, households, enterprises or public authorities, and rich and poor alike – markets are a means of empowerment.

It is not only in relation to individual transactions that failure to charge directly for goods and services, and to impose market tests, may bring welfare losses – and other damaging effects. In Britain today, goods and services provided by local authorities are largely financed from central government grants rather than local taxation. If local authorities mainly depended on revenue that came from taxes paid by their own voters, rather than on these centrally determined grants, they and the voters would behave more responsibly, balancing demands for services against acceptable tax levels. As in other market-based arrangements, consumers – in this case, local electorates – would be paying for what they demonstrably valued. At the same time, local authorities would no longer be cast as supplicants and lobbyists, while the central government would no longer be obliged to give time and resources to trying to supervise and control in detail the way they spend the grants made over to them.

The sphere of private business initiative can also be widened, again without formal transfer of ownership through privatisation, by permissive actions on the part of governments which relax prohibitions or controls. India provides a leading example of one form of prohibition, still in force: in relation to industrial policies, as noted in a recent article surveying the progress of

---

5   In a perceptive one-page note in *Economic Affairs*, 21(1), 2001, p. 47.

economic reforms, 'the main area where action has been inadequate relates to the long-standing policy of reserving production of certain goods for the small-scale sector'.[6] On a more positive note, in relation to China, Maddison writes that: 'There has been no formal reversion to capitalist property rights through privatisation of state property, but *de facto*, peasants have substantially regained control of their land, private house ownership is growing rapidly, and there is substantial scope for individual enrichment through private and quasi-private entrepreneurship' (*Chinese Economic Performance in the Long Run*, p. 61). The Chinese example illustrates the point that liberalisation which reinforces the primary role of business may shade into, and go together with, greater economic freedom for ordinary people: the new opportunities created are not necessarily restricted to companies (though of course people in general will gain from more effective corporate performance).

Business opportunities, and with them opportunities for ordinary people, may be restricted in other ways than through formal prohibitions and exclusions. A valuable recently published comparative study by the World Bank has thrown new light on (to quote the book's description) 'the scope and manner of regulations that enhance business activity and those that constrain it'.[7] The study covers 133 countries, and provides comparable information on them all. It focuses on five areas where business regulation may take effect: starting a business; hiring and firing workers;

---

6   Montek S. Ahluwalia, 'Economic Reform in India Since 1991: Has Gradualism Worked?', *Journal of Economic Perspectives*, 16(3), 2002, p. 72.

7   *Doing Business in 2004: Understanding Regulation*, a co-publication of the World Bank, the International Finance Corporation and Oxford University Press, 2003.

enforcing contracts; obtaining credit; and closing a business. For the world as a whole, it paints a picture of regulation as a serious constraining factor: the substantial body of evidence that it cites 'shows that in most countries government intervention is excessive and that it hurts business' (p. 93). The extent of over-regulation varies greatly across countries and legal regimes. Under all the five headings, generally speaking, those who might wish to set up and operate a business in accordance with legal requirements face greater procedural difficulties and delays, and higher costs of meeting the requirements, in poor countries than in rich ones. In large part, this results from regulation; but a further influence is that, especially in the more closely regulated countries, property rights are less clearly established and harder to enforce. The various handicaps thus imposed on business enterprises are reflected in lower output, restricted employment opportunities and slower economic progress: people in general are made worse off.

Besides the several aspects that are reviewed in this World Bank study, businesses are of course subject everywhere to various other forms of official regulation. In such a wide-ranging and complex area, generalisations are risky; but two statements can be made with some confidence.

First, in recent years there has in many countries been a trend towards deregulation of *particular industries* that had for long been highly regulated: among the leading instances are financial services, transport, telecommunications and power generation. This has been a leading aspect of the trend towards more market-oriented policies. There is ample evidence that, in most cases if not all, substantial benefits have accrued to consumers as a direct result of these changes. Again, the freeing or extension of retail opening hours has brought significant welfare gains in a number of previously regulated countries; and similar gains have been made in former communist countries where rationing and queues were pervasive under the old system. Under all these headings, despite what has been achieved, there remain in many countries further substantial possibilities for liberalisation. Second, and by contrast, there has also been, at any rate in most OECD member countries, a parallel trend towards tighter regulation of *businesses in general* under a number of headings, including taxation, environmental standards and occupational health and safety. In many cases, these actions have been taken without much regard for the probable balance of costs and benefits arising from them. It is true that some governments have recently shown awareness of the dangers of over-regulation. But there are strong tendencies in official regulatory agencies, often backed by courts and cheered on by many international agencies and NGOs, to view tighter regulations on commercially based activities as necessarily representing progress and to advocate cross-border uniformity as a general principle. A leading instance of such tendencies is the widespread uncritical endorsement of the 'precautionary principle'.

An area of regulation in which both individuals and institutions including businesses are closely involved is that of labour markets, where it is arguable that in virtually every country today both would gain, directly and substantially, from deregulation. The issues here go beyond those that are treated in the World Bank study just mentioned. As Richard Epstein has noted: 'Worldwide, the regulation of labor markets has created a legal edifice of stunning complexity. Protective laws abound on every conceivable aspect of the subject: health, safety, wages, pensions, unioniza-tion, hiring, promotion, dismissal, leave, retirement, discrimina-tion, access and disability.'[8]

In this area, a notable instance of over-regulation is again to be found in India, where (to quote Ahluwalia once more) 'any firm wishing to close down a plant or to retrench labor in any unit employing more than 100 workers can only do so with the permission of the state government, and this permission is rarely granted' (p. 76). In the OECD member countries, over the past forty years or so, there has been a gradual but cumulatively far-reaching extension of laws and official directives covering employ-ment-related matters. In Britain, a process which began in the mid-1960s has now brought with it over thirty Acts of Parliament or new sets of regulations, most of them dating from the past decade.[9] Instances of recently imposed restrictions in OECD coun-tries that are open to serious question, because of the constraints they impose on the freedom of choice of people and enterprises alike, include the legislation in France which now prescribes a 35-hour limit to the normal working week; the extension of protec-tive regulations to cover part-time as well as full-time workers, as in a recent EU directive; the trend towards tighter regulation to prevent 'unfair dismissals'; and the growth and spread of laws to further the related goals of 'anti-discrimination', 'equal opportu-nity', 'affirmative action' and 'diversity'.[10] Under these and other

8   Richard A. Epstein, *Simple Rules for a Complex World*, Harvard University Press, Cambridge, MA, 1995, p. 151.

9   A list of these is given on p. 22 of J. R. Shackleton, *Employment Tribunals: Their Growth and the Case for Radical Reform*, Institute of Economic Affairs, London, 2002.

10   In the latter context, a prime source is Richard Epstein's book *Forbidden Grounds: The Case against Employment Discrimination Laws*, Harvard University Press, Cambridge, MA, 1992.

headings, current regulations have the effect of compelling people and enterprises to enter into arrangements that they would prefer to avoid and narrowing the range of possibilities open to them. They impose standard rules and procedures which take little account of individual situations and preferences, and they are a fertile breeding ground for complexity, costly enforcement procedures, litigation, tensions and disputes. One way to strengthen the primary role of business, while directly benefiting individuals at the same time, would be to reverse the widespread erosion of freedom of contract that has taken place over recent decades and is still under way. The case for moving in this direction is stronger in so far as goods and services are produced and sold in competitive markets. In such markets, there is little scope for those who direct enterprises to act in ways that merely reflect prejudice, intolerance or inhumanity on their part, rather than concern for performance-related profits. Competition makes such ways of behaving a costly form of indulgence.[11] This is one of the benefits that a market economy brings with it, and a reason for widening its domain.

Liberalisation in context

Of course, and as emphasised already, economic policy has other aspects than those just referred to. Among these, and in particular, there are issues of distribution to be considered. The case for liberalisation, as summarised above, is stated in terms of the general welfare only, without regard to who may gain and who may lose

---

11   One study that develops this argument effectively, illustrating it by the case of South Africa in the days of apartheid, is W. H. Hutt, *The Economics of the Colour Bar*, Institute of Economic Affairs, London, 1964.

from the working of competitive markets or from changes that extend their scope. But the question of who gains and who loses from change is always of concern, to governments and voters alike, the more so if the losses appear as highly concentrated while prospective gains are widely diffused. A case can be made that liberalisation will be fairer, and certainly more acceptable, if it goes together with arrangements that provide forms of insurance, or even possibly forms of compensation, for those who lose from it. Hence measures to extend the scope of markets, and thus to strengthen the primary role of business, should (it is often argued) go together with complementary policies, which themselves are given shape and will take effect outside the market, to cushion the blow for those who suffer from the unforeseen changes that a dynamic economy gives rise to. An interesting recent variation on this latter theme is to be found in the recent book by Raghuram Rajan and Luigi Zingales, *Saving Capitalism from the Capitalists*.[12] While arguing forcibly the case for liberalisation, especially of financial markets, which they see as central to economic progress, the authors propose as one element in a fourfold strategy 'to foster free markets': 'A safety net … for the distressed, one that does not simply help the distressed cope with business cycle downturns but helps them bounce back from the complete loss of a career' (p. 294).

The design and operation of 'safety nets' forms one element only within a broader set of possible public initiatives. Governments everywhere are involved with issues of fairness and equality

---

12　Raghuram G. Rajan and Luigi Zingales, *Saving Capitalism from the Capitalists: How Open Financial Markets Challenge the Establishment and Spread Prosperity to Rich and Poor Alike*, Random House, London, 2003. Rajan is now director of the Research Department at the International Monetary Fund.

in ways that go well beyond the question of how to deal with the consequences of economic change. Moreover, these are arguably not just matters of reshuffling, of benefiting some by making others worse off. As the argument for safety nets suggests, the way in which issues of distribution are handled may in fact have a bearing on the prospects for economic progress, and hence on the welfare of people in general as well as that of particular groups. In this context, Angus Deaton, in a recent article, has made the general observation that 'According to a recent body of literature, equal societies have more social cohesion, more solidarity, and less stress; they offer their citizens more public goods, more social support, and more social capital; and they satisfy humans' evolved preference for fairness'.[13] Along these lines, one could think in terms of an egalitarian alternative (or complement) to the liberal approach, in which equality, rather than (or as well as) economic freedom, is viewed both as an end in itself and as a means to the realisation of other aims which include but go beyond prosperity. In any case, today as in the past, the main challenges to economic liberalism are made in the name of equality, social justice and human rights. It is true that economic progress and greater equality of incomes can go together.[14] All the same, economic freedom and economic equality are two different things, and the one may conflict with the other.

---

13 'Health, Inequality and Economic Development', *Journal of Economic Literature*, XLI, March 2003, p. 113.
14 A recent World Bank study of developing countries reached the conclusion that 'changes in the share of income that accrues to the poorest fifth of society are not systematically associated with the growth rate': hence (to quote the title of the study) 'Growth Is Good for the Poor'. The authors are David Dollar and Aart Kraay, and the study was published in 2001 as a World Bank Policy Research Working Paper.

The questions thus raised go well beyond the scope of this study. It is worth noting, however, that the case for liberalisation today, and for reinforcing the primary role of business, is not necessarily undermined if considerations of equality, poverty relief and fairness are taken into account.

Liberalisation and equality

For one thing, there are areas and initiatives within economic policy where equality is not and never has been a primary concern. Many of today's anti-liberal measures and policies are not designed to benefit poor people or poor countries: anti-dumping actions do not have this character, nor does the EU's damaging Common Agricultural Policy (CAP) and its counterparts in other OECD member countries, nor do regulatory norms and standards that have been made unreasonably complex or strict. Many of the liberalising initiatives listed above, under the headings of freer trade, privatisation and deregulation, would serve to change or replace arrangements which, whatever the benefits that can be claimed for them, have neither the intention nor the effect of reducing inequalities or relieving poverty. In such cases it is reasonable to focus primarily on the consequences of reform for the general welfare: liberalisation and equality are not in conflict.

The argument can be taken beyond such instances of compatibility. In some situations, the case for liberalisation can still stand even if reform is likely to make the distribution of income more unequal. For example, if the European Union were to abolish the CAP and adopt free trade for agricultural products, the world as a whole would be better off. A further result, however, could well be to increase the present wide gap in GDP per head between rich and poor countries, since the chief beneficiaries of the change would be people who are either rich or very rich by international standards. By far the greater part of the net gains would accrue to citizens of the EU itself, and the great bulk of the remainder to people in those agricultural exporting countries whose sales to the EU would increase significantly. Among these latter countries, some (the USA, Canada, Australia and New Zealand) count as very rich by international standards, while others (Argentina, Chile and Uruguay) have levels of GDP per head which are well above the world average. Though there would also be substantial gains to people in some poor countries, the gains to developing countries in general might not be proportionately so great as to their considerably richer counterparts. Hence although within the EU itself relatively poor people would gain from liberalisation more than their even richer fellow-citizens, the international distribution of income might become more rather than less unequal. But this is not an argument for keeping the CAP in place, still less for making it even more protective than it is today. In this case as in others, preoccupation with 'the gap' between rich and poor countries is misplaced.

A similar argument can apply when liberalisation within countries opens the way to greater general prosperity but brings with it greater inequality of incomes. China is a leading current example. The transformation of the Chinese economy in recent years has brought with it a widening of the gap in income per head between the richer and faster-growing regions, chiefly along the east coast, and much of the rest of the country. But the regions that have thus fallen farther behind are now much better off than they would have been if the old collectivist regime had survived, and this is what really counts. According to World Bank estimates, and on the bank's definition of the term, some 400 million people have emerged from poverty in China since the period of reform began at the end of the 1970s, while Surjit Bhalla, in the study referred to in Chapter 2, argues for a much higher figure. Moreover, the gap between regions would have widened less if liberalisation had been taken farther in China, by relaxing restrictions on internal migration.

In so far as the concern of policy is with poverty rather than inequality, the chief lesson of economic history, confirmed and reinforced by developments over the six decades since the end of World War II, is as stated above in Chapter 2: everywhere, the material progress of people, rich and poor alike, depends above all on the dynamism of the economies in which they live and work. The purpose and effect of liberalisation are to contribute to dynamism in those countries where the background conditions, as outlined in that chapter, are sufficiently realised for this to be possible.

Through reinforcing the primary role of business and widening opportunities for individuals and enterprises, enlarging economic freedom expands consumption possibilities for people in general: it clears a path for more rapid economic progress. It is therefore a positive-sum game. Granted, a similar argument can be made for equality, along the lines sketched out above in the quotation from Deaton. However, there are risks involved in emphasising equality as a goal. Measures or policies that are primarily redistributive, or which like many present-day labour market laws and regulations are designed to confer advantages on specific groups, are liable to be divisive zero-sum or negative-sum games. An ever-present danger is that they will focus the energies and attention of the many beneficiaries – whether individuals, households, businesses, industries, trade unions and professional bodies, social and occupational groups, local authorities, states or regions within a country, or countries within the European Union – on ways in which they can improve their own situation by making others worse off. Such a focus serves not only to reduce the likelihood of 'more social cohesion, more solidarity, and less stress', but also to retard economic progress.

A widely held view is that while competitive markets deliver prosperity, equity has to be pursued by other means. For instance, Amartya Sen has argued that: 'The far-reaching powers of the market mechanism have to be supplemented by the creation of basic social opportunities for social equity and justice'.[15] No one could reasonably object to the general idea that the 'powers of the market mechanism have to be supplemented'. But it would be wrong to imply that the existence and scope of markets, and the extent to which they are open and competitive, have little bearing on the availability of 'basic social opportunities'. Liberalisation down the years has served to create such opportunities, not only for Lang Hancock and his like, but also for the Chinese peasants and households that Maddison refers to in the quotations given just above and in Chapter 2, and for their counterparts elsewhere. All over the world, and in poor countries especially, the advancement of ordinary people largely depends today, as it always has, on the access to opportunities for employment and for personal and business initiatives, and on the ability to make choices, which economic freedom provides *both for them and for others*. It is not only through government and inter-governmental programmes

---

15 Amartya Sen, *Development as Freedom*, Oxford University Press, 1999, p. 143. In this study a much broader conception of freedom is developed than the one adopted here.

outside the sphere of markets that the cause of empowerment is served: freedom itself has a human face.

Improving capitalism: the respective roles of business and government

The purpose of liberalisation is to make capitalism function better, chiefly by harnessing profit-oriented businesses more closely to the general welfare. But in such a process the initiative does not rest with the business world. Enterprises themselves are not required to endorse or pursue the goal of improving capitalism along these lines, nor are they called on to act as partners in measures or programmes of market-oriented reform. The extent to which liberalisation is carried, and the directions that it takes, are determined by governments. In so far as capitalism is to be improved, and the primary role of business reinforced, by extending the scope of competitive markets, neither a change of heart nor a redefinition of roles is demanded on the part of businesses.

What if other objectives of policy, and with them other proposals for improving capitalism, are taken into account? Do businesses in this connection have scope today for making a stronger contribution of their own, and should the role and mission of enterprises be redefined accordingly? The doctrine of CSR gives positive answers to these latter questions. Its advocates believe that businesses have acquired the capability, and with it the duty, to ensure that capitalism now serves the goal of sustainable development: hence the case for 'corporate transformation'. By taking the path of CSR, business, working in new creative partnerships with governments and 'civil society', is seen as making capitalism anew.

This notion is based on a misreading of events and

relationships. It attributes to businesses new powers to influence outcomes which they have not in fact acquired. Thus when the authors of *Walking the Talk* refer (p. 60) to such issues as 'the developmental needs of the South' and 'the gap between the "haves" and the have-nots"' as now being on the agenda of businesses, they give a wholly unrealistic impression of what enterprises can achieve on their own account, even collectively. Now as in the past, the economic progress of poor countries does not depend on a commitment by companies to further it. As for the gap between 'the "haves" and the "have-nots"', it is governments alone which both retain the prime responsibility to decide whether and in what ways this is a problem and have the overwhelmingly greater capacity to address it. Now as in the past, it is governments, not businesses, which can influence the distribution of income through their power to regulate, to levy taxes, to pass social legislation, and to determine the level and composition of public expenditures. The same is true in relation to environmental issues and policies: it is for governments to assess situations and decide on action, and they alone have the power to give economy-wide effect, or even worldwide effect, to what they decide.

The advocates of CSR therefore greatly overstate the extent to which events and outcomes, and the degree to which objectives are realised, are influenced by what businesses decide. All the same, the extent to which the business world becomes committed to CSR is not a matter of indifference. As seen already, actions that reflect such a commitment can impinge on the general welfare, often in ways that are doubtful or damaging. In particular, businesses can make themselves subject to procedures that will raise costs; and they may become promoters of, or partners in, over-regulation of various kinds – for example, through the over-zealous pursuit of 'eco-efficiency', or by acting in ways that restrict employment opportunities in poor countries. In so far as such enterprise practices become general, they have a clear potential to do harm.

However, as noted in the previous chapter, the general voluntary adoption of CSR is unlikely to happen in an open and competitive market economy, where profit-oriented businesses are free to choose for themselves their objectives, strategies and ways of operating. In such a world, the vanguard firms will be subject to competition from nonconformers. It is only if the freedom of these nonconformers is restricted that the future of CSR can be assured. Here again, therefore, the role of governments is decisive. Capitalism cannot be made anew simply through the resolve of businesses themselves to embrace corporate citizenship and to act accordingly: to be sustained, the resolve of some has to be backed by regulations and sanctions that bear on all. Such measures, if fully effective, would indeed change the way in which capitalism operates, in particular by worsening the relative position of smaller enterprises and of firms operating in poor countries. By narrowing the scope of markets, they would weaken business performance of its primary role.

Business enterprises are at the heart of capitalism, but they do not determine its scope or character. Now as in the past, these are decided by governments. The conduct of businesses today, and the future of CSR, forms part of a wider complex of issues relating to the functioning and status of capitalism and the market economy and the extent of economic freedom. In the next and final chapter I consider the changing fortunes of capitalism and the market economy, and the main influences that bear on their prospects today, against the background of developments over the whole period since the end of World War II.

7 CAPITALISM, COLLECTIVISM AND BUSINESS: A 60-YEAR PERSPECTIVE

The fate of capitalism: flawed predictions

In his great book *Capitalism, Socialism and Democracy*, first published over sixty years ago and quoted in Chapter 2 above, Joseph Schumpeter reviewed both the past and the future of capitalism. As to the past, he pointed to the record of economic advances which had been made possible through the innovative role of business enterprises: he presented a picture of achievement. As to the future, he saw no good reason to assume or expect that capitalism would lose its momentum as a force for material progress. The main thesis of his book, however, was that (to quote from the preface to the first edition) '... a socialist form of society will inevitably emerge from an equally inevitable decomposition of capitalist society'. He took the view, not that capitalism would fail, but that it was 'being killed by its achievements'. The 'march into socialism', which he saw as already well under way, would continue inexorably, and bring with it 'the migration of people's economic affairs from the private to the public sphere ... a conquest of private industry and trade by the state' (4th edn, 1954, p. 408).

In the years following the end of World War II, there were obvious reasons for thinking that such a development was indeed well advanced and could be expected to continue. The war and events leading out of it brought a vast extension, in both Europe and Asia, of the area in which communist regimes held sway. Before long, the break-up of the former empires of leading capitalist countries led to the establishment of a host of newly independent states, chiefly in Asia and Africa; and in virtually all of these, beginning with India in 1947, governments were committed to socialism. Within the magic circle countries themselves, and still more in Latin America, capitalism was widely questioned, rejected or condemned. Alongside older criticisms to which it was subject, it was blamed by many for the chronic economic instability of the inter-war period and the calamitous Great Depression of the 1930s: it was seen as being no longer able to deliver.

Six decades on from the time when Schumpeter wrote, a very different set of outcomes has emerged from the one that he and many others foresaw.[1] Pessimists, fatalists and enthusiasts for radical change have alike been confounded. Capitalism has not disappeared from the scene, and few people now expect it to do so. Aside from a number of small economies, including Cuba, Libya and North Korea, there is no country in the world where, in the course of the whole period since the end of World War II, private industry and trade can be said to have been 'conquered' by the state. Why is it that, contrary to general expectations and the hopes of many, capitalism, and with it the role of private business,

---

1   Among leading economists who wrote on these issues around mid-century, Schumpeter was by no means the only one to see the future of capitalism as bleak. In an article published in 1961, Ludwig von Mises took the view that 'As ideological trends are today, one has to expect that in a few decades, perhaps even before the ominous year 1984, every country will have adopted the socialist system'. (The article is reprinted in a volume of Mises's essays entitled *Money, Methods and the Market Process*, published in 1990 by Kluwer Academic Publishers, Norwell, MA, and Dordrecht, where the quotation appears on p. 200.)

has emerged at the end of these six decades as more generally tolerated or accepted, and on the whole more securely established, than at the beginning?

The survival and re-emergence of the market economy

Both positive and negative influences have been at work. On the positive side, the main single factor has probably been the remarkable and unforeseen history of economic progress across much of the world over the second half of the twentieth century, as summarised in Chapter 2 above. How far this record of widespread (though not universal) economic achievement can be attributed to 'capitalism' as such is a matter of debate; and it is true that, broadly speaking, the contribution of business enterprises has not been given the recognition that it deserves. But almost all the countries concerned have had economies that were clearly market-based rather than centrally planned, while in some cases, with China since 1978 as the leading example, higher growth rates have been achieved as a direct result of policies that greatly widened the scope for private business initiative. Even though people in general did not necessarily give capitalism and business enterprises due credit for the successes, rising prosperity weakened the case for making fundamental changes in the system within which it was occurring. Rapid economic progress has brought acceptance of the market economy, though not necessarily enthusiasm for it, and has undermined the case for moving to, or keeping in place, a radically different socialist alternative.

A related factor has been the continuing role of business, and of private entrepreneurs, in innovation and hence in economic progress. First and foremost among the reasons that Schumpeter gave for thinking that capitalism would lose ground was that the entrepreneurial function was being eroded as a result of 'increasing mechanization of industrial "progress"'. He saw innovation as being increasingly the product of well-organised hierarchical research teams in large companies, rather than creative entrepreneurs: he held that, thanks to the very success of capitalism, the economic function of the business class 'tends to become obsolescent and amenable to bureaucratization' so that 'innovation itself is being reduced to routine'.

How far events have borne out this analysis is no doubt debatable; but I believe that even in relation to the advanced capitalist countries it appears as much too unqualified. A host of business episodes down to the present time, among them the development of the Pilbara iron ore mines, have given continuing evidence that the entrepreneurial role has by no means become obsolete. As to industrial or other bureaucrats taking over as innovators, an observation made by Alfred Marshall in the early 1920s is arguably still pertinent in the world of today. Reviewing the sources of future progress, Marshall emphasised the distinction between: '… tasks of orderly business management, which conscientious officials perform adequately; *and tasks of constructive enterprise, on the bold and enlightened discharge of which economic progress mainly depends*, though they are often beyond the powers of the official, and uncongenial to his temperament'.[2]

Further, and as noted in Chapter 2 above, it is mainly in the advanced capitalist economies, where enterprises are not too far away from the frontier of what is technically known and proved,

---

2   Alfred Marshall, *Industry and Trade*, Macmillan, London, 4th edn, 1923, p. 663. Italics added.

that the contribution of large research teams may often be critical to successful innovation. Schumpeter's whole analysis, reasonably enough, referred to the magic circle countries only. But the spread of modern economic growth to a growing range of countries outside the circle, and in particular the unforeseen and spectacular advances made in a number of previously poor Asian countries, has created new and substantial business environments whose shares in world output and trade have been rising fast; and as seen in Chapter 2 above, these environments typically provide ample opportunities for forms of business enterprise and initiative which are not primarily research-led. Innovation has not been reduced to bureaucratically-driven science-based routine in China or India today.

A third contributory influence, right through the period though with some slowing down in the troubled 1970s, has been closer international economic integration, and with it the extraordinary growth in cross-border trade and investment flows. Both official policies and technical advances including the recent revolution in communications have contributed to this internationalisation of the world economy. 'Globalisation' over almost six decades has greatly helped to extend the scope and improve the functioning of markets, and hence to improve economic performance; and together with the privatisations of recent years, it has opened up new opportunities for private businesses across the world.

During the 1970s, the market economy lost ground on balance across much of the world, as a result of economic setbacks and instability. In the OECD member countries, there was an obvious falling away in economic performance after 1973, as compared with the previous 25-year 'golden age'. This was widely taken as evidence of the basic weakness of capitalism, the more so because communist economies had experienced no such setback; and it gave rise to a range of interventionist measures and programmes. In many developing countries during the decade, there were further expropriations of foreign-owned businesses and extensions of public ownership. In China, this was still the era of the Cultural Revolution. But from the end of the 1970s onwards, as noted in the previous chapter, the trend toward collectivism was gradually and increasingly reversed. In a growing number of countries, economic policies became more market-oriented, the scope for private businesses was extended, and capitalism emerged as more accepted and less insecure than at any stage since the end of World War II.

These changes are often misdescribed and misinterpreted. As already noted, they did not establish a 'neo-liberal hegemony'. The trend to economic liberalism was far from universal, nor was it uniform or consistent in any of the countries where it appeared: everywhere, including in Britain and the USA, anti-liberal influences and tendencies persisted. Again, the shift in the balance of economic policies was not the natural continuation of some inexorable long-run trend towards greater economic freedom. On balance, and viewing the world as a whole, economic liberalism had been in retreat over the century that came to an end in the late 1970s. Last, the market-oriented reforms of the past 20 to 25 years were introduced by governments of widely varying political complexions: *they did not result from a general shift from left to right in the political centre of gravity, nor did they give expression to traditional conservative ideas and beliefs.*

While the story of these recent and unexpected market-oriented developments is a complex one, with many local themes and variations,[3] a leading influence almost everywhere has been disillusionment. Alongside the positive factors listed above, the survival and re-emergence of capitalism and the market economy have to be explained by the disappointing results or outright failure of experiments in public ownership and socialism. The most conspicuous instance of failure, and the most momentous in its consequences, has of course been the collapse of communism and of Soviet-style command economies. Less dramatically, and outside the former communist countries, disillusionment with the performance of public enterprises has been the main single factor in generating, and lending impetus to, the process of privatisation which has been taken a long way in a substantial and growing number of countries. Largely as a result of these twin developments, which again were not foreseen before the event, the market economy, over the past quarter of a century as a whole, has more than held its own. There has been a reverse 'migration' from the one that Schumpeter rightly perceived in his own day and understandably expected to continue and to prove irreversible: with respect to the ownership of enterprises, economic affairs have on balance moved back from the public to the private sphere.

Schumpeter opened Part Three of his book, which dealt with the socialist alternative to capitalism, by writing: 'Can socialism work? Yes, of course it can.' Few people today would echo this unqualified form of words.

Many commentators have drawn from these striking recent events the conclusion that (to quote one of them) 'the free market has emerged triumphant, accepted once again everywhere as the

---

3   The history is reviewed in Daniel Yergin and Joseph Stanislaw, *The Commanding Heights*, Simon and Schuster, New York, 1999, and in my own study, *The Changing Fortunes of Economic Liberalism*, already referred to.

natural condition of mankind'.[4] This is going much too far. In spite of its survival, the ground that it has gained and the discrediting of traditional socialist arguments and claims, the future of the market economy cannot be taken for granted. Even in the advanced capitalist economies of today, there remain strong and well-entrenched collectivist elements; and all over the world, hostility to market processes and private business is widespread. In no country is there a government, or even a political movement with strong support, which takes as a guiding principle the case for greater economic freedom. The future of capitalism has still to be assessed against a background of suspicion, questioning and distrust, which recent corporate failures and scandals have served to reinforce. Collectivist views and anti-market pressures remain influential everywhere, and for many of those who hold such views the collapse of communism might just as well have taken place on another planet. Despite its recent gains, the future scope and status of the market economy are by no means assured. They are put in question by the powerful combination of beliefs, influences and pressures which I have termed *new millennium collectivism*.

The power of new millennium collectivism[5]

In the still-flourishing collectivism of today, several mutually reinforcing elements are to be seen. Interests and pressures, doctrines

---

4   Oliver Letwin, MP, 'Civilised Conservatism', in *Conservative Debates*, Politeia, London, 1999. Letwin is now 'Shadow' Chancellor of the Exchequer and the leading spokesman on economic affairs for the British Conservative Party.
5   In this and the following section I have drawn in part on my 2000 Wincott Lecture, *Anti-Liberalism 2000: The Rise of New Millennium Collectivism*, Institute of Economic Affairs, London, 2001.

and ideas, are alike involved. The two spheres, of thought and action, are often interconnecting; and both are affected, sometimes decisively, by events and perceptions of events. Many of the influences at work are long-established if not timeless: it is the millennium which is new, rather than present-day collectivism as a whole. But as emphasised in Chapter 4 above, some distinctively new collectivist elements have gradually emerged and taken hold in recent years. Among these latter, two related tendencies stand out. One is the emergence of the NGOs as a force in the world, while the other is the increasing hold of global salvationist ideas. As a result of these developments, traditional and still-thriving collectivist influences have increasingly become linked to, and reinforced by, global salvationist thinking and programmes of action.

One ever-present influence on policies – age-old, though it constantly takes new forms and finds new outlets – is the pressures that come from interest groups concerned to promote their economic advantage, either by safeguarding existing protective and restrictive arrangements or through acquiring new favours, concessions and benefits from governments. The origins and effects of such pressures form the leading theme of Mancur Olson's remarkable book *The Rise and Decline of Nations*: Olson's thesis is that 'the behavior of individuals and firms in stable societies leads to the formation of dense networks of collusive, cartelistic and lobbying organizations that make economies less dynamic and polities less governable'.[6] Often, though by no means always, the strongest and most effective pressures of this kind have come

---

6   Mancur Olson, *The Rise and Decline of Nations: Economic Growth, Stagflation, and Social Rigidities*, Yale University Press, New Haven, CT, 1982. The quotation is from the dust jacket.

from within the business community. In today's context, this latter aspect is strongly emphasised and well brought out in the study already referred to, by Rajan and Zingales, so much so that their book is entitled *Saving Capitalism from the Capitalists.* They focus on the ways in which (to quote from the dust jacket of the book) 'Powerful interest groups oppose markets, especially financial ones, because markets undermine their positions'.

While the threats to the market economy that Rajan and Zingales point to are real, I believe that their analysis of the forces at work is incomplete. They overstate the extent to which interest group pressures originate from businesses; focus too exclusively on pressures that reflect economic motives; give too little weight to the point – though they acknowledge it – that business economic pressures may be directed towards market opening, rather than restriction; and in particular, underrate the extent to which the collectivism of today derives support from ideas rather than interests, or from both in conjunction.

As to the first of these points, many of the current pressures to restrict the sphere of markets do not come from established businesses with defensive motives, but from non-business institutions and groups, and even ordinary people, who wish to maintain or secure benefits and special treatment for themselves, or for those they represent, through the agency of public authorities. Prominent among the institutions are local authorities and central government spending departments, acting on behalf of interests and causes which are not at all confined to businesses. Among the non-business lobbyists and beneficiaries are local taxpayers and an array of actual or potential recipients of transfers, grants, benefits, special assistance, and free or subsidised provision. In the UK, a homely illustration of such activities is provided by the political process in Wales. In a recent election there the local Labour Party leader, following the well-marked path for rulers exemplified in the tale of Good King Wenceslas, fought a successful campaign 'pledging to abolish prescription charges and offering free breakfasts at primary schools, free home care to the elderly, and ... free admission to public swimming baths for children and pensioners' (*The Times*, 3 May 2003, p. 17). Such withdrawals of goods and services from market provision may be prompted not only by redistributive aims, but also by the well-established tendency to extend the notion of 'public goods' to areas of spending, such as routine healthcare and university education, where the description is questionable or inappropriate.

Such straightforwardly economic interests are not the only ones involved. The anti-liberal pressures of today do not arise just from the direct pursuit of monetary gain or advantage, whether by business or non-business interests: organisational goals may also play a part. For example, two sources of influence in the modern world, both significant and often complementary, are first, the pressures for collective action brought to bear by anti-market 'public interest' NGOs, and second, the chronic propensity on the part of many government departments and international agencies to favour closer regulation, often in ways that do not reflect, or which go directly against, the preferences of business. These working alliances between officials and NGOs form a distinctively recent influence, though their origins can be traced back some three decades or more.

Capitalist interest groups, therefore, are by no means the only significant source of anti-market pressures and lobbying; and indeed, they can, when it suits them, act as determined advocates of market opening. The case of iron ore mining in Western

Australia is a clear example. The pressures from Lang Hancock and his business allies in the 1950s and early 1960s, on both the Commonwealth and the Western Australian governments, were directed towards getting rid of official restrictions and prohibitions on market-based activities: although their actions were of course profit-motivated, they were campaigning, in their particular area of concern, for greater economic freedom. It would not be difficult to find parallel instances for such business campaigns today – for example, in advocating further privatisation, and favouring the principle of national treatment in relation to foreign direct investment. Again, as Martin Wolf rightly points out (*Why Globalization Works*, p. 311), 'the rise of the internationally integrated transnational company has reduced the ability (and willingness) of producers to wrap themselves in national flags', and oriented them towards market opening rather than old-style national protectionism.

The story of Australian iron ore exports also provides a copybook illustration of a pervasive influence on events and policies which economists, and others too, are inclined to overlook or play down. The pressures for maintaining the statutory export prohibition did not at all arise from material interests, whether business or non-business: *they arose from mistaken economic arguments and assumptions*. The main assumption was that Australian resources of iron ore were strictly limited; and the inference drawn was that the Commonwealth government should ensure that these scarce resources were reserved for future exclusively Australian use. Despite their obvious flaws, these arguments were accepted uncritically in official circles, technical and political. Policy was determined, not by interest group pressures or opportunist vote-catching by politicians, but by what were wrongly seen as the merits of the case. The governments concerned were guided by their conception of the public interest.

This episode is one of the countless instances, ancient and modern, in which economic policies have been influenced or decided by firmly held intuitive economic ideas and beliefs which owe little or nothing to textbooks, treatises or the evidence of economic history. These various notions can justly be termed 'pre-economic'. I class them together under the heading of 'do-it-yourself economics' (DIYE). All over the world, as each day's news bears witness, they retain their hold over people and their power to influence events.[7]

As this past Australian example shows, what is in question here is not just 'popular economic fallacies', the uninstructed beliefs of unimportant people. To the contrary, leading ideas that go to make up DIYE are sincerely held, and voiced with conviction, by political figures, top civil servants, CEOs, general secretaries of trade unions, well-known journalists and commentators, religious leaders, senior judges and eminent professors. That is why they have to be taken seriously as an influence on events. This is not 'pop economics', since it is embraced by leaders as well as the led; it is not 'voodoo economics', since those who practise it are not just cranks; and it is not 'businessmen's economics', since its adherents are equally to be found in other walks of life.

---

7   Evidence as to the character, pervasiveness and influence of DIYE, together with many specific instances of it, can be found in my short book *Innocence and Design: The Influence of Economic Ideas on Policy*, Blackwell, Oxford, 1986, as also in pp. 121–7 of *The Changing Fortunes of Economic Liberalism*. A prize specimen of highly influential DIYE fantasy, referred to on pp. 44–5 of the London edition of *The MAI Affair*, was the best-selling book published in 1967 by the French author Jean-Jacques Servan-Schreiber, *Le Défi Américain*, brought out in English translation as *The American Challenge*, Hamish Hamilton, London, 1968.

Some characteristic long-established DIYE notions have already made their appearance in earlier chapters. The oldest and perhaps the most influential of these is the belief, or assumption, that actions undertaken for profit, or more broadly for reasons of self-interest, are open to question as such. This typically goes together with an intuitive mistrust of markets: they are seen as anarchic and disruptive, as well as amoral, if not driven by sinful greed. An observation made about socialists in a recent book by Anthony de Jasay applies more broadly to today's exponents of DIYE, many of whom might not wish to describe their views as socialist – namely, that they ' ... tend to speak of the "market" as though it were a person, and a downright dangerous character at that, inclined to malignant deeds. They make accusations against the "market" that they would never make against the "set of voluntary exchanges", overlooking that these two are synony-mous of each other.'[8] Another characteristic feature of DIYE, likewise noted above, is a collectivist vision of economic change, in which the material progress of ordinary people chiefly depends, not on the growth of productivity and output per head through investment and innovation, but on deliverance from above. One aspect of such deliverance is regulation to protect workers against what are taken to be chronically and ruthlessly exploitative profit-oriented enterprises which, if left unregulated, would have the power to impose terms and conditions of employment of their own choosing and to give free rein to prejudice and intolerance in their treatment of different groups.

Such firmly held intuitions are linked with others that also

---

8   Anthony de Jasay, *Justice and Its Surroundings*, Liberty Fund, Indianapolis, IN, 2002, p. xxiii.

point in a collectivist direction and can be mutually reinforcing. Among these is what I term 'unreflecting centralism', that is, the attribution to states and governments of roles, powers and functions which are not necessarily theirs. One aspect of this centralism is the belief, or presumption, that when transactions take place across national boundaries the state is necessarily involved, so that cross-border economic competition is between states. This belief provides a rationale for interventionist trade and industrial policies, the more so when combined with the mercantilist conviction that exports are to be counted as a gain to a country and imports as a cost. Another common DIYE presumption is that goods and services and activities can be usefully classified as either essential or non-essential, or, in a more refined taxonomy, ranked in order of priority. In either case, it is the responsibility of governments to ensure essential supplies or to see that priorities are enforced.

In today's DIYE, some already established ways of thinking have been given a more topical flavour. The resulting notions include several that have already been referred to above: that reducing 'the gap' between rich and poor, often greatly overstated when international comparisons are in question, should be a primary concern; that the goods and services available to humankind are made available by Planet Earth and unjustly pre-empted by people in the rich countries; that in a market economy the progress of ordinary people is dependent, in the absence of redistributive measures, on a not-to-be-relied-on process of 'trickledown'; and that recent globalisation has 'marginalised' poor people and poor countries and shifted the power to act and decide from governments to MNEs. To this list has now been added the more far-reaching presumption that the great majority of the world's population, and not just the poor and the employed, are actual or potential victims, whose status as such can be remedied only by actions on the part of 'society'. All these notions fit well with the prevailing alarmist beliefs and assumptions relating to population, resources and the environment, and the supposedly dire consequences of economic activity, that were likewise outlined above in Chapter 4: the newer or refurbished elements in DIYE form an integral part of today's global salvationism. In turn, salvationism itself fits well with, and is reinforced by, some older staple elements of DIYE, such as unreflecting centralism and the conviction that good results can reliably flow only from conduct that is not based on self-interest.

While interests and ideas are often separate influences, they can be especially effective when mutually reinforcing. Pressure groups typically carry weight not just through skilful lobbying and persuasion directed towards those in power, but also by winning assent or support from a wider public opinion which sees the objectives in question as fair, reasonable or in the national interest. Indeed, without such public support, or at any rate acquiescence, interest groups are unlikely to achieve their aims. Now as in the past, many of the strongest interventionist pressures arise from the combined influence of DIYE and the lobbies.

Collectivist groupings and alliances

Within the ranks of modern collectivists, there are disparate and sometimes warring elements. A radical or militant wing comprises four main categories:

- 'deep green' environmentalists, who wish to assert the rights of other living creatures, and of the earth as a whole, against what they view as the damaging and destructive activities of human beings;

- radical egalitarians, whose concern is to put an end to a whole range of differences and disparities perceived as unjust;
- all-out anti-globalists, who favour a return to what appears to be a modern version of the medieval manorial economy;
- postmodernists who reject what they see as today's dominating culture of transnational capitalism.

Despite their differences, these groups broadly share a vision of the world in which past history and present-day market-based economies are characterised by systematic oppression and abuses of power. Free markets and capitalism are seen as embodying and furthering environmental destruction, male dominance, racial intolerance, class oppression, imperialist coercion and colonialist exploitation. Such attitudes have been little affected by the collapse of communism. Although the groups that hold them are not well represented in the corridors of power, they are by no means insignificant. Among their members all have votes, many are active and vocal, and some are well represented through NGOs.

Alongside the radicals, and in some cases and on some issues in sympathy with them, are the informal, wide-ranging and influential combinations of forces that make up modern mainstream anti-liberal thinking and action. Both interests and ideas are involved, often in conjunction. The groupings and alliances may extend to businesses and business organisations, trade unions, the more moderate NGOs, academics from a range of disciplines, commentators and public figures including parliamentarians, political leaders and civil servants, government departments, an assortment of interventionist quangos, and virtually all UN agencies, presumably with the sanction of their member governments. These are not participants on the margin of events, but coalitions that can draw on wide official and unofficial support.

One reason for the attraction of such alliances, and their breadth of membership, owes more to ideas than to interests. Both radical and mainstream critics of capitalism render allegiance today to three highly appealing interrelated concepts. Two of these, which have been mentioned already, are sustainable development and corporate social responsibility. The third is 'positive' human rights. All three appear, and are presented, as inherently proof against doubts or objections: who could want to oppose, deny or restrict human rights, to prefer that corporations should act non-responsibly, or to advocate development that would be unsustainable? Yet all these virtuous-seeming notions, as now interpreted, bear a collectivist message.[9]

New millennium collectivism is not a fringe phenomenon: it is by no means confined, as Martin Wolf suggests in two friendly references to my use of the term, to 'the groups who unite to protest against global capitalism'.[10] The collapse of communism has not done much to weaken its influence; and within the core

---

9   On aspects relating to the interpretation of human rights, a useful critique of current orthodoxy is Bernard Robertson, *Economic, Social and Cultural Rights: Time for a Reappraisal*, New Zealand Business Roundtable, Wellington, 1997.

10   *Why Globalization Works*, pp. 3 and 312. Because he focuses so strongly on this particular aspect of today's collectivism, I believe that Wolf gives too rosy a picture of the current situation and future prospects of economic liberalism. It is not only the radical opponents of global capitalism who stand for collective and regulatory 'solutions'.

OECD countries in particular, it has arguably gained ground over the past ten to fifteen years. To be sure, today's radical critics, who wish to overthrow capitalism, no longer have a coherent alternative to offer. To that extent, the market economy has indeed prevailed, and its future appears secure. But businesses and profit-motivated activities are still suspect in the eyes of many if not most people, while anti-market ideas, beliefs and pressures not only remain pervasively influential, in ways that have been little affected by the manifest failure of full-blooded socialism, but have gained ground as a result of the growth and spread of global salvationism. A continuing threat to the market economy thus arises, not just from anti-capitalist groups and movements on the periphery, but also, and principally, from mainstream opinion of various kinds in conjunction with a wide range of unceasing interest group pressures.

Giving way to anti-liberalism: lapses in business and government

One reason why anti-liberal influences have held or gained ground in recent years is the inability, reluctance or failure on the part of two sets of key institutions within the OECD member countries to counter them. One of these twin instances is to be found in the business world, while the other lies within governments.

Within the *business* milieu of today, a striking feature is the extent to which anti-market and anti-business arguments, claims and assertions as to the facts have not only gone largely unchallenged, but have been uncritically accepted and endorsed by corporations, business leaders, business organisations, and business authors and commentators. Instances have been quoted above, and a good deal of further evidence is presented in *Misguided Virtue*. In this earlier study, I noted (p. 58) that:

> ... many large corporations that have come out for CSR, whether directly or through organisations which they have created and continue to finance, have lent support to ideas and beliefs that are dubious or false. On behalf of business, they have been ready to endorse uncritically ill-defined and questionable objectives; to confess imaginary sins; to admit to non-existent privileges, and illusory gains from globalisation, that require justification in the eyes of 'society'; to identify the demands of NGOs with 'society's expectations', and treat them as beyond question; to accept over-dramatised and misleading interpretations of recent world economic trends and their implications for businesses; and in some cases, to question outright the economic system of which private business forms an integral part.

Since this was written, further evidence of the same ways of thinking has emerged, as illustrated in some of the excerpts quoted above from *Walking the Talk*.

CSR is indeed, as it claims to be, a radical doctrine, more so in fact than its advocates typically realise: it involves outright rejection of principles that form the basis and rationale of a market economy. It offers a new conception of the role and status of business enterprises. It assigns to all businesses new primary goals, defined with reference to what are taken to be 'society's expectations', in place of enterprise profitability, which becomes no more than a consequence of, and a means to, the pursuit of these goals. It links the endorsement of 'corporate citizenship' and 'sustainable development' to new and more elaborate operating procedures for enterprises. As part of these procedures, it makes firms accountable, not just to their owners, but to an array of 'stakeholders'; and as Elaine Sternberg has noted (*Corporate Governance: Accountability in the Marketplace*, op. cit., p. 134), this is 'incompatible with good corporate governance'. It points towards tighter regulation, whether formal or informal, to ensure that all businesses conform to its precepts. Further, it puts forward claims on behalf of businesses and other NGOs for forms of participation in 'global governance' which if conceded would weaken democratic accountability. Both in itself and for the non-business company it keeps, it is to be counted among the many anti-liberal influences of today.

In taking this collectivist path, the various business elements involved have of course been part of a broader movement of opinion: CSR is a child of our time. It is perhaps not surprising that the ideas prevailing in business circles have been influenced by a view of the world so widely held as that of global salvationism. It is worth noting, however, how little the business milieu has done to inform and improve the prevailing climate of opinion relating to the range of questions considered in this study. With few exceptions, the recent contributions to public debate on these issues that have been made by corporations and the business world generally, and pro-CSR businesses and business organisations in particular, do little credit to those holding positions of responsibility within them.

Within *governments*, interventionist notions and pressures are often to be found, not surprisingly, in many specialised ministries – for example, those dealing with environmental, trade, labour market and other regulatory issues. What is more surprising, and less commented on, is the part played – or not played – by the central economic departments of state. These comprise treasuries, ministries of finance or economics, and, in some countries, specialised agencies such as the US Council of Economic Advisers. While their chief responsibilities relate to macroeconomic issues and public finance, they can also have a wider role. It is with these departments and agencies that the coordinating function in economic affairs within governments resides, if indeed it resides anywhere. Only they have a legitimate claim, if they choose to exercise it, to review the whole spectrum of a government's economic policies, and to try to bring to those policies a measure of order and consistency. Only they can try to ensure that an informed and reasonably consistent economic approach is brought to bear across the spectrum.

In relation to the issues considered here, none of these departments has succeeded in defining such an approach and making it effective, nor is it clear that any of them have made a serious attempt to do so. A leading instance of this neglect, already touched on in Chapter 4 above, is the treatment of economic issues in relation to the work of the Intergovernmental Panel on Climate Change. In noting the critique of the IPCC process that Ian Castles and I had put forward, referred to above, an article in *The Economist* (8 November 2003, p. 96) made the pertinent comment that: 'You might think that a policy issue that puts at stake hundreds of billions of dollars' worth of global output would arouse at least the casual interest of the world's economic and finance ministries. You would be wrong.' Throughout its life, the IPCC itself, its parent UN agencies and the departments within its member governments which it reports to have been left by those governments to handle economic issues as they think fit, with results that appear to have gone unquestioned and indeed unnoticed by 'the world's economic and finance ministries'.

This is just one leading example of a continuing lack of resourcefulness on the part of these same ministries, which can be traced back at least as far as their failure to give due attention to the Rio Summit of 1992. On a variety of fronts, the central economic departments of state in OECD member countries have largely failed to resist, or even to take cognisance of, the growing influence of anti-business and anti-market NGOs; the global salvationist and anti-market line taken by the great majority of international agencies; the uncritical endorsement by their own governments of questionable notions of 'sustainable development', 'social exclusion', 'global governance' and 'Corporate Social Responsibility'; and the substantial and continuing erosion of freedom of contract through intrusive laws and regulations. They have surrendered large areas of ground to collectivist ideas and pressures, with serious implications for the general welfare, without effective resistance, and indeed without fully realising what has been going on.

The orientation of policies

Given the continuing power of collectivist pressures and beliefs, future moves towards more collectivised and interventionist economic systems are not difficult to imagine, despite the broadly market-oriented tendencies of the past 20 to 25 years. It is true that, in view of the generally recognised failure of both central planning and public ownership of business enterprises, there is no reason to expect that the trend to privatisation will be reversed. There is still ample scope for other anti-liberal measures and programmes, however. The previous chapter sets out a number of headings under which liberalisation could now be taken farther;

and the same list, with the omission of privatisation, can serve as the headings under which policies could move in the reverse direction. Anti-liberal lines of action could thus include: raising barriers to international flows of trade and foreign investment; increasing the scope and raising the levels of public transfers, in ways that further loosen the connection between rewards and market-directed economic activity; further 'demarketisation' of goods and services which are not authentic 'public goods', through free or heavily subsidised provision; and maintaining or intensifying, over a range of areas, current trends towards increasingly strict and intrusive regulation. Under this last heading would come official actions designed to make the adoption and implementation of CSR by business enterprises obligatory.

All such tendencies, while not presenting a threat to capitalism as such, would narrow market opportunities and reduce competitive pressures. All of them can be viewed as real and continuing possibilities in the world of today: there are few countries where initiatives of this kind can be ruled out, or even viewed as improbable.

On the other side of the balance, there are today, and operating in most countries including all the largest economies, forces and influences which serve to keep competitive markets open and promote their further extension. Some of these influences arise from markets themselves: they include continuing technical advances, especially in communications; the growing internationalisation of transactions and of business operations; the widespread awareness of what has been achieved in the advanced capitalist countries; and – as ever – the wish of people and enterprises everywhere to create and exploit opportunities for making themselves better off. As to official policies, there are clear market-oriented tendencies and possibilities to be seen around the world.

For example, privatisation can be expected to continue, and has a huge potential still, in economies that include China and India; many governments have shown awareness of the possibility and dangers of over-regulation, and some are acting accordingly; the trend towards unilateral liberalisation of international trade and investment flows could well be taken farther in some developing and transition countries; and some of these flows may likewise become freer as commitments made in the Uruguay Round come into effect and regional integration is taken farther in some parts of the world. Moreover, the tendency for governments to give way to pressures for higher transfers and subsidies, or new forms of free provision, is often held in check, and can even be reversed, by the resistance of taxpayers. For all these reasons, anti-liberal tendencies, even if significant, may be outweighed by moves in the opposite direction.

The future balance between liberal and anti-liberal elements, and even the overall direction of change, are of course uncertain. Now as always, there are no fated or readily predictable outcomes; and in pondering the future evolution of capitalism, and the policies that will bear on it, a new element of uncertainty has now entered the equation. Until recently, and as in Schumpeter's day, it was reasonable to consider the situation and prospects of capitalism with reference only to the magic circle countries. But other important centres of capitalist enterprise have now grown up, in an astonishing way, in countries that were previously poor and in some cases highly collectivised. In particular, the future of capitalism and the market economy now have to be considered with reference to developments in China and India, and these may take a different path from that which has been followed historically in the core OECD countries.

For the present purpose, fortunately, neither predictions nor scenarios are required. It is reasonable to take as working assumptions, first, that economic regimes and policies across the world will continue to embody both liberal and anti-liberal elements, though the mix will no doubt differ over time and across countries; second, that such a mix is likely to be found within areas of policy, such as international trade or labour markets, as well as overall; third, that neither element will necessarily be dominant at all times, in all places, and across the whole range of policies; and fourth, that the various anti-liberal elements, as outlined above, may often be significant even where they are not dominant. These possible future developments have to be seen in relation to a point of departure today in which, as seen already, regimes and policies everywhere contain strong and well-established collectivist features even though recent trends in policy have on balance been liberal.

Capitalism secured?

How far do widespread and influential collectivist beliefs, pressures and tendencies, current and prospective, represent a threat to capitalism and the market economy? Two rival answers to this question can be given, one reassuring from a liberal standpoint and the other more sombre. Both have good arguments on their side.

On the former interpretation, there is a clear and fundamental division between capitalist and socialist economic systems, and it is socialism only that presents a significant threat to capitalism and economic freedom. Viewed in relation to this sharp divide between the two systems, intra-system differences are not a serious matter. There are admittedly different variants of capitalism, some more regulated and state-directed than others, but all are distinctively capitalist; and while not all socialist economies are identical, they too bear a family likeness. Hence it is questionable, if not wrong, to think of a continuum of arrangements in which increasingly regulated capitalism merges into the milder forms of socialism. There is no blurred frontier, but rather a well-marked dividing line. Capitalism has indeed triumphed in recent years, as a result of the collapse of communism; and the question of just how interventionist different capitalist regimes are now, or may be in course of becoming, is of second-order importance. The point is that they are not socialist.

Such a thesis has been persuasively developed by Janos Kornai, who had ample opportunity to observe socialism at close quarters as a resident of Hungary under the former communist regime.[11] He presents socialism and capitalism as the only economic systems now existent: 'the 20th century has not given rise to a third system' (p. 30); and he draws a clear line between their respective 'system-specific attributes'. He lists the three critical differences, which themselves give rise to others, as being:

- under socialism, the Marxist-Leninist party has undivided power; under capitalism, political power is 'friendly to private property and the market';
- under socialism, state and quasi-state property are dominant; under capitalism, private property has a dominant position;

---

11   Janos Kornai, 'What the Change of System from Socialism to Capitalism Does and Does Not Mean', *Journal of Economic Perspectives*, 14(1), winter 2000. This article is based on the same author's study, *From Socialism to Capitalism: What Is Meant by the 'Change of System'?*, Social Market Foundation, London, 1998.

- socialism is characterised by 'bureaucratic coordination', capitalism by 'market coordination' (p. 29).

This comparison has to be viewed in the light of a further distinctive property of the socialist system which Kornai describes (p. 31) as follows: 'The original transition to socialism did not arise by organic development: the socialist system does not originate spontaneously from the intrinsic, internal forces of the economy. Instead, the socialist system is imposed on society by the communist party with brutal force, when it gains power.' On this view, therefore, socialism will almost certainly not be introduced in a functioning democracy – though Kornai does allow later (p. 40) for the possibility that the people of some former communist countries, disillusioned with capitalism as they have now experienced it, will voluntarily choose to restore a socialist order of some kind. Equally, however, these latter countries are now free to choose 'the version of capitalism that they prefer'. Their choice could well be a version that emphasised fairness and equality, as well as economic freedom, as in the German 'social market economy'.

This analysis points to a reasonably assured future for both capitalism and the market economy. It suggests that, in most of today's world, the only forms of collectivism that are seriously harmful to freedom, economic progress and the primary role of business no longer hold sway and are unlikely to return. Capitalism has indeed won the day. The extent to which different forms or variants of capitalism reflect concerns other than economic freedom will continue to be a matter for debate, but it is not one of fundamental choice.

Capitalism collectivised?

By contrast, an alternative and less sanguine view can be taken of the status and prospects, not so much of capitalism as such, but of the market economy and economic freedom. The argument can be summarised as follows.

It is true that authoritarian socialism has been discredited, so that it no longer appears as a serious rival to capitalism. But this change on the world scene has left unaffected the deep-rooted and long-established collectivist features of today's capitalist economies, especially though by no means only in the core OECD countries. Collectivist ideas and presuppositions in these and other countries have not been weakened by the failure of command economies, since those economies were never viewed, except by unrepresentative fringe groups, as a model to be imitated. Within today's OECD member countries, established collectivism continues to find expression – most notably in continuing forms of selective protectionism; in high levels of public expenditure and tax revenue in relation to GDP, largely because of redistributive programmes; and in the growth and spread of regulation. Collectivist tendencies have remained in evidence in recent years, alongside the various market-oriented reforms such as privatisation which have admittedly been a countervailing influence, and they can be expected to persist. Nor is there a clear fire-break which will prevent such tendencies from leading to some form of socialism since, to quote the view expressed in a recent book by Thomas Sowell: 'Despite the sharp distinction in principle between government-planned economies and market economies, in reality there is a continuum between the two'.[12]

---

12   Thomas Sowell, *Applied Economics: Thinking Beyond Stage One*, Basic Books, New York, 2004, p. 22.

An author who consistently stressed the dangers for capitalism and the market economy *from developments arising within it* was F. A. Hayek. In a late work, for example, he refers to the 'progressive increase of coercive discrimination [which] now threatens to strangle the growth of a civilization which rests on individual freedom'.[13] The possibilities which he thus pointed to are not now closely linked, as in the past, to authoritarian regimes and the absence or suspension of democracy: to the contrary, they arise from the way in which collectivist tendencies and pressures continue to manifest themselves, alongside and notwithstanding the recent economic reforms, in the democratic capitalist economies of today. The essential point here is well made by Anthony de Jasay in *Justice and Its Surroundings* (p. 281): 'The issue of freedom in our civilization is changing its character. It is not so much despots, dictators or totalitarian creeds that menace it. In essence, we do.'

According to this view of the world, then, Soviet-style socialism has indeed been discredited, perhaps for good; but it does not follow that the market economy has emerged as triumphant, or even as predictably secure, since entrenched Western-style collectivist thinking, which neither endorsed nor borrowed from the Soviet model, has retained its hold on public opinion, and its influence on economic policies, across the world. The actions that result are a matter for concern, not just because they make people in general poorer, but also, and still more, because they represent a threat to freedom and opportunity.

---

13   F. A. Hayek, *Law, Legislation and Liberty*, Routledge, London, one-volume edn, 1982. The above quotation is from p. 129 of Volume 3, entitled *The Political Order of a Free People*. By 'discrimination' Hayek means here actions designed to benefit particular interests or groups at the expense of everyone else.

Such arguments appear as all the stronger when account is taken of the rise of global salvationism, which has given new impetus to collectivist thinking and proposals for action in ways that were not fully anticipated by authors such as Hayek.

The future of the market economy

How worrying are existing forms of anti-liberalism, and the possibility of their gaining ground in the ways just outlined? Is Kornai correct in suggesting that the choice between different variants of capitalism, and the relative emphasis that they place on economic freedom and equality, are not fundamental issues, or is Hayek to be taken seriously when he refers to 'strangling the growth of a civilisation which rests on individual freedom'? I believe that Kornai is right to emphasise the gulf between authoritarian socialism and any of the various forms of capitalism that exist, or may evolve, in modern democratic countries. But this is not the whole picture. While Hayek's sombre vision may be over-dramatic, the choice between different possible variants of capitalism, some more 'socialised' or collectivised than others, is not at all a minor matter.

It is of course true that preferences as between more and less market-directed variants may reflect legitimate differences with respect to values, objectives and facts: there is plenty of room for debate here. Initiatives and policies that their critics label as 'anti-liberal' or 'collectivist' may be viewed by others as well-judged means to achieving generally agreed aims – through remedying market failure, providing genuine public goods, dealing with the environmental consequences of under-regulated economic activity, or giving effect to widely shared concerns relating to fairness and equality. But while this is true, it is also true that, now as in the past, many measures and policies which restrict the scope of competitive markets arise from the pressures and persuasive powers of particular interest groups, from beliefs and presumptions that are largely or wholly unfounded, or from a combination of both. There is no reason to expect that actions that result from these influences, and thus reflect a varying blend of special interest lobbying and basic misconceptions, will serve well the causes of prosperity, fairness or freedom.

Granting that many collectivist initiatives can be damaging, there is still a question as to how serious their consequences are likely to be. Those who take a relaxed view of the future of the market economy would not deny that some initiatives and policies which restrict the scope of markets do more harm than good; but they consider that, at any rate in the capitalist economies of today, such effects are relatively minor and likely to remain so. For one thing, there are liberal as well as anti-liberal trends and influences in these economies, and over the past 20 to 25 years the former have been on balance in the ascendant. More fundamentally, reassurance can be seen as justified by the sheer resilience of capitalism, the market economy and profit-oriented businesses – their well-demonstrated capacity to function to good effect within the sphere permitted to them, despite the presence of exclusions, regulations, restrictions and pressures which limit that sphere. Even if dubious anti-market interventions should gain ground on balance in the coming years, which is by no means certain, capitalism (it can be argued) can be expected to survive, to spread farther, and to continue to provide the basis for economic progress at historically high rates. Viewed in this light, Hayekian-type concerns about a threat to civilisation appear as greatly overdone.

Though this line of thought is not mistaken, it is likewise not the whole picture. Even if it is accepted, the case for further liberalisation remains valid. More fundamentally, such arguments give too little weight to the range and severity of existing anti-liberal policies and measures, and the possibility that some of them at least will be intensified. To a substantial though unquantifiable extent, today's pervasive and mutually reinforcing modes of anti-liberalism – protectionism, over-regulation, exclusion of goods and services from the market, and focusing of the energies and ingenuity of people and organisations on securing gains for themselves at the expense of others – reduce welfare and act as a drag on economic progress. It is true that, in countries where the background conditions of public order and stability are satisfied, rapid progress can now be generally counted on despite these influences. But this is itself due in large part to the way in which market economies have spread and become freer over the past half-century or more, while the prospects for future advances, in poor countries as well as rich, will be improved in so far as liberalisation is now taken farther, along the lines sketched out in the previous chapter.

It is not only prosperity and economic progress which are in question. The case against measures and policies that narrow the scope of markets and reduce economic freedom does not rest only on the damaging effects that they are liable to have on the material welfare of people in general. They may also impair or degrade the quality of individual and social life, in ways that do not show up in measured consumption of goods and services.

One instance of such effects is to be found in international economic relations. It now appears likely that discriminatory bilateral and regional trade agreements will not only grow in number, but will incorporate as a regular feature provisions relating to environmental and labour standards in the poorer countries that are party to them. Insistence on such provisions is worrying primarily because, as noted in Chapter 3 above, they are liable to narrow the scope for mutual gains from trade and direct investment and restrict employment opportunities in poor countries. But in addition, they turn what could be low-level arm's-length transactions between people and enterprises, freely engaged in, into matters of high-level and potentially divisive inter-governmental negotiation. Such demands as are now made on poorer countries by both the USA and the EU are liable to become a source, not only of disintegration and impoverishment within the world economy, but also of needless international friction and disorder.

A further and related possibility, likewise touched on in Chapter 3 above, arises from currently proposed innovations in 'global governance'. The forms of 'participatory democracy' and 'popular sovereignty' that are now widely advocated by NGOs and their allies, including not only a range of UN agencies but also many international corporations and business organisations, would weaken representative democracy and the status and accountability of national governments. They bring with them the risk of what has been termed a 'power shift to the unelected'.[14]

Within national boundaries, a topical instance of the damaging effects of recent collectivist initiatives, in this case on the quality of institutions, is the relentless and still continuing decline of British universities. This is chiefly due to the way in which successive British governments of both major parties, from

14   The phrase forms the subtitle of a study by Marguerite Peeters, entitled *Hijacking Democracy*, published in 2001 and accessible on the website of the American Enterprise Institute at <www.aei.org>.

the 1980s onward, have chosen to give effect to the unfounded notion that undergraduate education is to be viewed as meeting national needs for qualified manpower, and hence is properly treated as a quasi-public good to be provided increasingly widely and financed almost entirely from public funds. The ensuing demands for 'accountability' have given rise to new or intensified forms of central government intervention, including in particular a plethora of performance and 'quality' indicators covering all aspects of teaching and research. These latter impose heavy burdens on academic and other staff, and distort incentives; and in conjunction with the marked downward trend in real funding per student, they have brought a reduction in the quality of the undergraduate learning experience.

Probably the most worrying single aspect of recent and current anti-liberal tendencies is the closer regulation of labour markets and contracts of employment. It may well be that the full effects are still to be seen of increasingly comprehensive and detailed laws, regulations and mandatory working practices adopted in the name of anti-discrimination, equal opportunities, 'diversity', 'core standards', and 'positive human rights'. As noted in the previous chapter, the already established array of regulations across the world, in addition to its consequences for freedom of choice and material welfare, is a fertile source of complexities, concealment and dissimulation, tensions, resentments, disputes and litigation.[15] Here as in some other areas, measures that are seen as

---

15 Further harmful effects of the same kind can be confidently predicted for a current European proposal in this area, by which the present draft constitution for the European Union would confer on employees the right to 'lifetime training'. Despite its high-level sponsorship, this idea bears the stamp of irresponsibility. It illustrates well the risks attendant on extending indefinitely the sphere of 'positive' human rights.

giving expression to 'solidarity' are in fact deeply and congenitally divisive.

The argument concerning the wider harmful effects of today's collectivism can also be put in a positive way. Just as limiting the scope of markets can impair the quality of life, in a wide variety of ways, so the enlargement of economic freedom can enhance it. Such possibilities are overlooked by those who view markets, and transactions within them, as no more than a means to providing tangible goods and services. A recent instance of this latter way of thinking is to be found in an article by Mohan Munasinghe, a prominent figure in the councils of the IPCC, where he is vice-chair of the panel's Working Group III. The article is entitled 'Analysing ethics, equity and climate change in the sustainomics trans-disciplinary framework'.[16] Munasinghe takes as given the accepted partitioning of 'sustainable development' into three distinct domains – economic, environmental and social – and comments (p. 92) that: 'The economic system is geared mainly towards improving human welfare (primarily through increases in the consumption of goods and services). ... The social system seeks to enrich human relationships and achieve individual and group aspirations.' There is here a false antithesis. It is wrong to contrast an economic system which provides for material wants and purchases with a social system which enables other and loftier goals to be fulfilled. It is not just for its contribution to material welfare that economic freedom is to be valued. The freedom of people and lawful associations of all kinds to spend their money and dispose of their property as they wish; to choose

---

16 The article forms the fourth chapter of a book of essays entitled *Ethics, Equity and International Negotiations on Climate Change*, edited by Luiz Pinguelli-Rosa and Mohan Munasinghe, Edward Elgar, Cheltenham, 2002.

their lifestyles, occupations, lines of business and places of work; to trade and remit funds freely across political boundaries, and within them, to travel without restriction and choose where to live and operate; to decide how and where to invest their time and resources; to determine for themselves what products and services to produce and sell, and on what terms; and to enter without restriction into voluntary arrangements and contracts for mutual benefit – all these are means not only to higher consumption of goods and services but also to a fuller, more creative, more cooperative and more interactive life. The effect of economic freedom is precisely 'to enrich human relationships and achieve individual and group aspirations'. It is not only outside or despite the market economy that people are able to act in ways that will make their lives more complete, as well as materially richer. The two aspects are not separate, and it is on account of both that the choice between different systems and arrangements, all of which can formally be classed as 'capitalist', is not to be viewed as a minor matter. Today's collectivist influences and tendencies may not pose a threat to capitalism; but they can reduce economic freedom, and weaken the primary role of business, in ways that cause impoverishment of more than one kind.

ABOUT THE IEA

The Institute is a research and educational charity (No. CC 235 351), limited by guarantee. Its mission is to improve understanding of the fundamental institutions of a free society with particular reference to the role of markets in solving economic and social problems.

The IEA achieves its mission by:

- a high-quality publishing programme
- conferences, seminars, lectures and other events
- outreach to school and college students
- brokering media introductions and appearances

The IEA, which was established in 1955 by the late Sir Antony Fisher, is an educational charity, not a political organisation. It is independent of any political party or group and does not carry on activities intended to affect support for any political party or candidate in any election or referendum, or at any other time. It is financed by sales of publications, conference fees and voluntary donations.

In addition to its main series of publications the IEA also publishes a quarterly journal, *Economic Affairs*.

The IEA is aided in its work by a distinguished international Academic Advisory Council and an eminent panel of Honorary Fellows. Together with other academics, they review prospective IEA publications, their comments being passed on anonymously to authors. All IEA papers are therefore subject to the same rigorous independent refereeing process as used by leading academic journals.

IEA publications enjoy widespread classroom use and course adoptions in schools and universities. They are also sold throughout the world and often translated/reprinted.

Since 1974 the IEA has helped to create a world-wide network of 100 similar institutions in over 70 countries. They are all independent but share the IEA's mission.

Views expressed in the IEA's publications are those of the authors, not those of the Institute (which has no corporate view), its Managing Trustees, Academic Advisory Council members or senior staff.

Members of the Institute's Academic Advisory Council, Honorary Fellows, Trustees and Staff are listed on the following page.

The Institute gratefully acknowledges financial support for its publications programme and other work from a generous benefaction by the late Alec and Beryl Warren.

Other papers recently published by the IEA include:

WHO, What and Why?
Transnational Government, Legitimacy and the World Health Organization
Roger Scruton
Occasional Paper 113; ISBN 0 255 36487 3
£8.00

The World Turned Rightside Up
A New Trading Agenda for the Age of Globalisation
John C. Hulsman
Occasional Paper 114; ISBN 0 255 36495 4
£8.00

The Representation of Business in English Literature
Introduced and edited by Arthur Pollard
Readings 53; ISBN 0 255 36491 1
£12.00

Anti-Liberalism 2000
The Rise of New Millennium Collectivism
David Henderson
Occasional Paper 115; ISBN 0 255 36497 0
£7.50

Capitalism, Morality and Markets
Brian Griffiths, Robert A. Sirico, Norman Barry & Frank Field
Readings 54; ISBN 0 255 36496 2
£7.50

A Conversation with Harris and Seldon
Ralph Harris & Arthur Seldon
Occasional Paper 116; ISBN 0 255 36498 9
£7.50

Malaria and the DDT Story
Richard Tren & Roger Bate
Occasional Paper 117; ISBN 0 255 36499 7
£10.00

A Plea to Economists Who Favour Liberty:
Assist the Everyman
Daniel B. Klein
Occasional Paper 118; ISBN 0 255 36501 2
£10.00

The Changing Fortunes of Economic Liberalism
Yesterday, Today and Tomorrow
David Henderson
Occasional Paper 105 (new edition); ISBN 0 255 36520 9
£12.50

The Global Education Industry

Lessons from Private Education in Developing Countries
James Tooley
Hobart Paper 141 (new edition); ISBN 0 255 36503 9
£12.50

Saving Our Streams

*The Role of the Anglers' Conservation Association in
Protecting English and Welsh Rivers*
Roger Bate
Research Monograph 53; ISBN 0 255 36494 6
£10.00

Better Off Out?

The Benefits or Costs of EU Membership
Brian Hindley & Martin Howe
Occasional Paper 99 (new edition); ISBN 0 255 36502 0
£10.00

Buckingham at 25

Freeing the Universities from State Control
Edited by James Tooley
Readings 55; ISBN 0 255 36512 8
£15.00

Lectures on Regulatory and Competition Policy

Irwin M. Stelzer

Occasional Paper 120; ISBN 0 255 36511 X

£12.50

Misguided Virtue

False Notions of Corporate Social Responsibility

David Henderson

Hobart Paper 142; ISBN 0 255 36510 1

£12.50

HIV and Aids in Schools

The Political Economy of Pressure Groups and Miseducation

Barrie Craven, Pauline Dixon, Gordon Stewart & James Tooley

Occasional Paper 121; ISBN 0 255 36522 5

£10.00

The Road to Serfdom

The Reader's Digest *condensed version*

Friedrich A. Hayek

Occasional Paper 122; ISBN 0 255 36530 6

£7.50

Bastiat's _The Law_
Introduction by Norman Barry
Occasional Paper 123; ISBN 0 255 36509 8
£7.50

A Globalist Manifesto for Public Policy
Charles Calomiris
Occasional Paper 124; ISBN 0 255 36525 X
£7.50

Euthanasia for Death Duties
Putting Inheritance Tax Out of Its Misery
Barry Bracewell-Milnes
Research Monograph 54; ISBN 0 255 36513 6
£10.00

Liberating the Land
The Case for Private Land-use Planning
Mark Pennington
Hobart Paper 143; ISBN 0 255 36508 x
£10.00

IEA Yearbook of Government Performance 2002/2003
Edited by Peter Warburton
Yearbook 1; ISBN 0 255 36532 2
£15.00

Britain's Relative Economic Performance, 1870–1999
Nicholas Crafts
Research Monograph 55; ISBN 0 255 36524 1
£10.00

Should We Have Faith in Central Banks?
Otmar Issing
Occasional Paper 125; ISBN 0 255 36528 4
£7.50

The Dilemma of Democracy
Arthur Seldon
Hobart Paper 136 (reissue); ISBN 0 255 36536 5
£10.00

Capital Controls: a 'Cure' Worse Than the Problem?

Forrest Capie

Research Monograph 56; ISBN 0 255 36506 3

£10.00

The Poverty of 'Development Economics'

Deepak Lal

Hobart Paper 144 (reissue); ISBN 0 255 36519 5

£15.00

Should Britain Join the Euro?

The Chancellor's Five Tests Examined

Patrick Minford

Occasional Paper 126; ISBN 0 255 36527 6

£7.50

Post-Communist Transition: Some Lessons

Leszek Balcerowicz

Occasional Paper 127; ISBN 0 255 36533 0

£7.50

A Tribute to Peter Bauer

John Blundell et al.

Occasional Paper 128; ISBN 0 255 36531 4

£10.00

Employment Tribunals

Their Growth and the Case for Radical Reform

J. R. Shackleton

Hobart Paper 145; ISBN 0 255 36515 2

£10.00

Fifty Economic Fallacies Exposed

Geoffrey E. Wood

Occasional Paper 129; ISBN 0 255 36518 7

£12.50

A Market in Airport Slots

Keith Boyfield (editor), David Starkie, Tom Bass & Barry Humphreys

Readings 56; ISBN 0 255 36505 5

£10.00

Money, Inflation and the Constitutional Position of the Central Bank

Milton Friedman & Charles A. E. Goodhart

Readings 57; ISBN 0 255 36538 1

£10.00

Corporate Governance: Accountability in the Marketplace
Elaine Sternberg
Second edition
Hobart Paper 147; ISBN 0 255 36542 X
£12.50

The Land Use Planning System
Evaluating Options for Reform
John Corkindale
Hobart Paper 148; ISBN 0 255 36550 0
£10.00

Economy and Virtue
Essays on the Theme of Markets and Morality
Edited by Dennis O'Keeffe
Readings 59; ISBN 0 255 36504 7
£12.50

Free Markets Under Siege
Cartels, Politics and Social Welfare
Richard A. Epstein
Occasional Paper 132; ISBN 0 255 36553 5
£10.00

Unshackling Accountants

D. R. Myddelton
Hobart Paper 149; ISBN 0 255 36559 4
£12.50

The Euro as Politics

Pedro Schwartz
Research Monograph 58; ISBN 0 255 36535 7
£12.50

Pricing Our Roads

Vision and Reality
Stephen Glaister & Daniel J. Graham
Research Monograph 59; ISBN 0 255 36562 4
£10.00

To order copies of currently available IEA papers, or to enquire about availability, please contact:

Lavis Marketing
IEA orders
FREEPOST LON21280
Oxford OX3 7BR

Tel: 01865 767575
Fax: 01865 750079
Email: orders@lavismarketing.co.uk

The IEA also offers a subscription service to its publications. For a single annual payment, currently £40.00 in the UK, you will receive every title the IEA publishes during the course of a year, invitations to events, and discounts on our extensive back catalogue. For more information, please contact:

Subscriptions
The Institute of Economic Affairs
2 Lord North Street
London SW1P 3LB

Tel: 020 7799 8900
Fax: 020 7799 2137
Website: www.iea.org.uk